THE
RULE OF
30

THE
RULE OF
30

A BETTER WAY TO SAVE
FOR RETIREMENT

FREDERICK VETTESE

Published by ECW Press
665 Gerrard Street East
Toronto, Ontario, Canada m4m 1y2
416-694-3348 / info@ecwpress.com

Editor for the Press: Jennifer Smith
Cover design: David A. Gee
Author photo: Dean Macdonell

Care has been taken to trace ownership of copyright material contained in this book. The author, editor, and publisher welcome any information that enables them to rectify any reference or credit for subsequent editions.

The information presented herein represents the views of the author as of the date of publication. Because market conditions, laws, regulations, and procedures are constantly changing, the examples given are intended to be general guidelines only and the author reserves the right to alter and update his views based on new conditions as they develop. The information and opinions contained herein should not be construed as being official or unofficial policy of any government body or agency.

The material in this publication is provided for information purposes only. This publication is sold with the understanding that none of the author, the editor, or the publisher is hereby rendering specific professional advice. If professional advice or other expert assistance is required, the services of a competent professional should be sought.

This book is also available as a Global Certified Accessible™ (GCA) ebook. ECW Press's ebooks are screen reader friendly and are built to meet the needs of those who are unable to read standard print due to blindness, low vision, dyslexia, or a physical disability.

Purchase the print edition and receive the eBook free. For details, go to ecwpress.com/eBook.

LIBRARY AND ARCHIVES CANADA CATALOGUING IN PUBLICATION

Title: The rule of 30 : a better way to save for retirement / Frederick Vettese.

Other titles: Rule of thirty

Names: Vettese, Fred, 1953- author.

Identifiers: Canadiana (print) 20210208953 | Canadiana (ebook) 20210208988

ISBN 978-1-77041-617-8 (softcover)
ISBN 978-1-77305-833-7 (ePub)
ISBN 978-1-77305-834-4 (PDF)
ISBN 978-1-77305-835-1 (Kindle)

Subjects: LCSH: Retirement income—Canada—Planning. | LCSH: Finance, Personal—Canada.

Classification: LCC HG179 .V485 2021 | DDC 332.024/0140971—dc23

The publication of The Rule of 30 is funded in part by the Government of Canada. Ce livre est financé en partie par le gouvernement du Canada. We also acknowledge the support of the Government of Ontario through Ontario Creates.

Canadä

PRINTED AND BOUND IN CANADA

PRINTING: MARQUIS   5   4   3   2   1

To Gregory, Troy, Michael and Alex

TABLE OF CONTENTS

LIST OF TABLES AND FIGURES

LIST OF ACRONYMS

The various retirement-related acronyms that are used throughout the text are all shown here, along with the chapter in which they first appear.

CPI   Consumer Price Index for Canada (Chapter 2)

CPP   Canada Pension Plan (Chapter 2)

CRA   Canada Revenue Agency (Chapter 5)

CCB   Canada child benefit (Chapter 4)

DB   defined benefit, as in DB pension plan (Chapter 9)

DC   defined contribution, as in DC pension plan (Chapter 7)

EI   Employment Insurance (Chapter 4)

ERP   equity risk premium (Chapter 18)

ETF   exchange-traded fund (Chapter 9)

OAS   Old Age Security, usually in reference to OAS pension (Chapter 2)

QPP   Quebec Pension Plan (Chapter 1)

P/E   price to earnings (ratio) (Chapter 18)

PERC   Personal Enhanced Retirement Calculator (Chapter 6)

RESP   Registered Education Savings Plan (Chapter 7)

RRSP   Registered Retirement Savings Plan (Chapter 1)

FOREWORD

To say things have changed over the last few decades would be an understatement. For the most part, these changes are right before our eyes in the form of smartphones, connected cars, streaming content and nearly unlimited information at our fingertips. But some changes are not so obvious.

Consider saving for retirement. Between defined benefit pensions and high risk-free interest rates, preparing for retirement used to be easier from the individual's perspective. Unfortunately, defined benefit pensions are now virtually extinct, at least in the private sector, and real interest rates are essentially non-existent.

Among employers who do offer pension plans, the move from defined benefit to defined contribution plans has transferred much of the onus to individuals; and for the far too many Canadians who have no workplace coverage at all, the responsibility of saving for retirement is entirely theirs. This leaves the average individual more at the mercy of the capital markets than ever before. To see how this sea change affects saving for retirement, we must shed some old assumptions and look more closely under the hood. More than that, we must look closely at ourselves and our habits if we are going to be able to overcome the new financial challenges we face.

As the founder of Purpose Investments, cofounder of WealthSimple and someone who has dedicated my life to making investing more structured and accessible to Canadians, it goes without saying that I strongly believe in the importance of saving for retirement. This is what has attracted me to Fred's thinking and work over the years. I have always found Fred to have a clear perspective on the challenges we face, as a society and as individuals, in thinking about and preparing for retirement.

But how do we get this clear thinking into the hands of every Canadian and then help them implement it? This book is a great start, whether you are a young professional beginning your career, or if you have just gotten over the daycare hump and your kids are now at the point where they are starting to realize you are not as cool as they once thought.

This book neatly frames the problem many young Canadians face in trying to figure out how much they should save each year. People generally understand that this is something important to do, whether it is an afterthought following the purchase of a home or a luxury item or a conscious question they ask themselves after they receive their first paycheque. But answering the question can involve so many variables that the task can feel overwhelming. With the time for retirement so far in the future, it is much too easy to defer answering the question until it is too late.

For most people, successfully saving for retirement is a matter of forming good habits. To do that, the importance of saving must be recognized and acted upon. And the earlier you do this the better, because time is your greatest ally in achieving your retirement goals. You do not even need to have specific goals to get started saving. You can decide how to live and spend your money further down the road. But if you do not save, you will not have many options.

"The Rule of 30," as Fred describes, solves this problem by providing a very thoughtful yet easy-to-follow framework for young Canadians. It allows them to take the first step to begin saving for retirement, regardless of their financial situation. The framework is flexible and adjusts to your life stage, taking into consideration both your current and potential future salary and expenses.

Once you are much closer to retirement, you will need to look more closely at your overall financial situation to define your retirement goals and to ultimately understand if you are ahead, on track or behind schedule for meeting them. When you reach that point you can make the appropriate tweaks, if required. But without a base of retirement savings gradually built up over the years, there will be nothing to tinker with and retirement may be an elusive goal.

Another hurdle to overcome is the expectation for returns on fixed-income securities. Thirty years ago, you could count on a 7 percent income in retirement simply through buying high-quality bonds. Today, that same portfolio would garner a return of under 2 percent, likely earning a negative return when inflation is taken into consideration.

One of the most dangerous things we can do when it comes to saving is to assume that what has worked in the past will work in the future. Commentators have been predicting a return to higher interest rates for years. As Fred argues in this book, it may be a very long time before that materializes, so we need to adjust our retirement and saving plans to present-day realities.

The Rule of 30 considers the current macro-economic environment and provides new ways for young Canadians to approach their asset allocation today. It is a valuable tool in helping to change the perception of retirement saving, as Fred offers new ways to approach the problem and build a solution. With Fred's advice and insights, saving for retirement is easier than ever.

Get ready to take control of your situation and get started on ensuring you are on the right path to a well-planned and secure retirement.

SOM SEIF

FOUNDER AND CEO OF PURPOSE INVESTMENTS

PART I

Lessons from the Past

CHAPTER 1

How Much Should You Save?

Deciding how much to save for retirement sounds like a question that should have a ready answer, and yet, there is no apparent consensus. Ask different retirement experts and they will give you starkly different responses, or else none at all. While some variability is to be expected from one person to the next, surely there should be a rule of thumb.

Despite their obvious shortcomings, good rules of thumb have their uses. They resonate with people who do not have the time or interest to become subject experts. If a specific rule doesn't put them on precisely the best path, it at least ensures they do not stray too far.

I started on my quest for the ideal percentage to save by asking a group that I call "the Shed."[1] This is an informal group of now-retired pension luminaries (nearly all of them actuaries) who meet regularly to discuss the state of the world. When it comes to retirement issues, they once commanded the attention of Canada's biggest employers, both public and

---

[1]   Like any cabal, they prefer to remain behind the scenes. But here are their initials: BC, DE, MH, JN, HN and DS.

private. I reasoned that if anyone could tell me how much we should be saving, it would be them.

Not surprisingly, they were reluctant to grace such a vague question with a response, so I provided a little more context. I made it known that I was seeking the percentage of pre-tax income that youngish adults should be saving on a regular basis if they wished to retire comfortably at an age that most of us would regard as "normal." To avoid groupthink, I asked each person to give me their responses independently. If they all gravitated to the same number, I told myself, then maybe I could end my search. I will provide their answers later in this chapter. In the meantime, I decided to investigate what other knowledgeable sources were saying.

Rob Carrick of the *Globe and Mail* reminded me that a rule of thumb already exists and is quite well-known. In David Chilton's classic book, *The Wealthy Barber*, he suggested that people save 10 percent of their pay year in and year out. But that was 30 years ago. Since then, risk-free real interest rates have fallen from more than 4 percent to negative territory. Also, the Canada/Quebec Pension Plan (CPP/QPP) has been expanded and retirement patterns have changed. With all those moving pieces, it seemed unlikely that Mr. Chilton's simple recommendation would have remained unaltered. And did Canada's big financial institutions — banks, life insurance companies and investment firms — ever buy in to the 10 percent target in the first place?

I went to the banks to find out, and quickly discovered them to be enormously reluctant to endorse any one figure. If you google "saving for retirement in Canada," the Bank of Montreal (BMO) comes up before the other banks, so I have to assume they are trying especially hard to be a major player in the retirement saving arena. Yet, there is no mention anywhere on their website of what percentage of pay one should set aside for retirement. They do suggest that savers "max out" on their RRSP contributions, and they conveniently offer loans to make this happen. But there is no saving percentage anywhere in sight.

The same goes for Scotiabank, who informed me they do not promote any particular saving rate, but they did suggest that people should save enough to produce retirement income of 60 to 80 percent of their final average employment earnings. More on that later.

I had only slightly better luck with RBC. My source couldn't find anything in the company's promotional material that resembled a rule of thumb, although he did mention that he had come across "passing references to a 10 percent figure, but the language around them is non-committal."

Since the banks weren't terribly helpful, I proceeded to look in less obvious places. One of them was an impressive-looking website maintained by an arm of the federal government known as the Financial Consumer Agency of Canada. That website contains a wide array of useful tips and insights to savers under the heading "Saving for Retirement." What they don't have is an actual saving percentage recommendation.

Moving on, it seemed reasonable to think that the Ministry of Finance might be a good source of information. They must have a view on the appropriate saving rate, given that the Income Tax Act dictates how much one can save for retirement on a tax-assisted basis. Under that Act, the contribution limit to an RRSP is 18 percent of pay.[2] Maybe I could take this as a first approximation of what one official body regards as the "right" saving rate?

On the other hand, 18 percent is the *maximum* they allow, which they know few Canadians ever reach on a regular basis, so surely the right answer in their eyes must be less than 18 percent. Or is it? The very people who originally created this 18 percent limit — federal civil service employees — participate in a pension plan where the contribution rate is 20 percent of pay[3] *at a minimum* and can be considerably higher should a deficit arise.

Other big public-sector pension plans like the Ontario Municipal Employees' Retirement System (OMERS) and the Ontario Teachers' Pension Plan (OTPP) also require contributions of at least 20 percent of pay. This is in spite of their having sophisticated investment management teams that can supposedly achieve significantly better returns than the average person. Has the right percentage to save truly risen to 20 percent?

It is only fair to point out that some respected subject experts do cite percentages within the many retirement planning books that are out there, but their message appears not to have registered with the public at large. (The irony of that observation is not lost on me.)

---

2   It is subject to a dollar limit, which we can ignore here. The dollar limit is only there to cap the revenue that CRA loses by allowing tax-deductible contributions.

3   Employer and employee combined.

By this time in my search, I was running out of places to look, at least in Canada. My last find was an online article by Global News, which reported that "you may have heard you should be saving 10–15 percent of your pre-tax income." This was tantalizing, since I wasn't sure I *had* heard that, though it did sound vaguely familiar. Alas, this little nugget turned out to be little more than hearsay. The article didn't cite the source of this 10–15 percent range or attempt to confirm that it is indeed correct. It smacked of urban legend. It was at this point that I gave up on Canada.

Curiously, US sources proved to be much more forthcoming with tangible recommendations, and quite aggressive ones at that. On their website, Fidelity recommends that you save 18 percent a year for your entire career if you start at age 30. If you wait until 35 to start saving, they advise you to be saving 23 percent a year. Charles Schwab cites similar numbers. Start saving in your 20s, they say, and 10 to 15 percent may be enough (or maybe not). Wait until 45, and you might need to save as much as 35 percent.

T. Rowe Price recommends saving at least 15 percent a year, but their promotional material implies you should be doing this starting in your 20s, so presumably it contemplates a 40-year-long stretch of saving. I did the math and estimated that this equates to saving 28 percent of pay if you start in your 30s and save for a "mere" 30 years.

All three of these companies also suggest that the retirement income target should be 70 to 80 percent of one's final average pay, which may explain the high saving rates they recommend. (I would note in passing that Fidelity, Schwab and T. Rowe Price all make more money when everyone saves more.) These are daunting numbers; high enough to make a 30-year-old despair and not even try to save, which may explain why so many Americans have barely saved anything at all for retirement.[4]

What is the correct answer, then? Is it 10 percent of pay like Mr. Chilton originally suggested? Has it slowly migrated up to 15 percent in this low-interest era? Or could the public-sector pension plans be right to think one should sock away 20 percent or more? It was time to go back to my mini-survey of the Shed and see what this august body had for me.

---

4   A Northwestern Mutual study shows that one in three have saved less than $5,000 and one in five have saved nothing at all.

Here are the six responses I received (all expressed as a percentage of pre-tax income): 20 percent, 20 percent, 20 percent, 10 percent, 10 percent and 9 percent. So, there you have it. We are no closer to a universal percentage than we were at the outset.

Is it possible I was asking the wrong question? Rather than seeking a universal percentage of pay, perhaps the real holy grail is a better process for saving. In these pages, we will explore this idea as well as a number of other concepts. We will do so through the eyes of a young couple, Brett Thompson, 33, and Megan Leigh, 30, who are also looking for answers.

By way of background, Brett always had a soft spot for redheads, and he fell instantly for Megan when they met at their former place of work. She ultimately reciprocated his feelings and before too long they got married. Both have good jobs and good prospects for advancement, and both plan to continue working after they start having children. Last year, Brett and Megan bought their first home. Even though it was well outside the city, the purchase strained their financial resources. The down payment alone consumed all of their hard-earned savings as well as the small inheritance Megan received when her father died a few years ago. They financed the rest with the biggest mortgage they felt comfortable in taking on.

Now that they have their home, the next financial hurdle is saving for retirement. Even though retirement seems eons away, everyone tells them it is best to start saving early to benefit from the magic of compound interest. Fortunately for Brett and Megan, their next-door neighbour, Jim, is a retired actuary with time on his hands and answers in his hip pocket. He is about to lead them on a financial odyssey.

CHAPTER 2

It Was the Worst of Times

Saturday, May 29

On a beautiful Saturday morning in late spring, Brett happened to be outside his house, where Megan had put him in charge of cleaning windows. Brett spied his neighbour Jim over the hedge separating their properties and casually started what could be one of the most important conversations of his life.

"Hi, Jim. Your roses are looking good."

"Thanks," said Jim, eyeing Brett intently. Over 30 years of working with clients told him that Brett had something on his mind besides roses.

"Jim, do you mind if I ask you a question?" asked Brett.

"Sure, fire away."

"Well," continued Brett, somewhat sheepishly, "can you give any advice on how much Megan and I should be saving for retirement?"

"Hmm. It depends on a lot of things, such as how the stock market does, future trends in interest rates and when you plan to retire. Not to mention inflation, tax rates and what might happen to government pension benefits. Now . . ."

Jim stopped in mid-sentence when he saw Brett glazing over. It had been a few years since Jim had retired from the pension business, but his consulting instincts were still sharp, and they told him he was losing his audience quickly.

Changing tack, Jim asked, "Tell me, when were you thinking of retiring? Not soon, I hope."

Brett chuckled at that. "In about 30 years. At that point, I'll be 63 and Megan will be 60."

"Ah yes, Megan," said Jim. "We should definitely include her in any discussion on saving for retirement. The answer is not going to be as simple as you might like, and it's something you both should hear. Tell you what, let me finish pruning my roses and if you're both free later today, we can resume our discussion."

Brett's face lit up. "Great! Shall we say four o'clock? Why don't you come to our place and we'll fix you a drink?"

"See you then."

At precisely 4 p.m., Brett and Megan heard the doorbell. When they answered, they saw Jim with a laptop case in one hand and a file folder in the other. Jim followed their gaze to the laptop and explained, "I brought along a few things to help illustrate what I'm going to tell you."

They settled in the living room. Brett furnished the promised drink, and Jim immediately got down to business.

"Basically, you want to know how much you have to save to retire 30 years from now. Presumably your goal is to be able to continue the same lifestyle you had just before retirement, while you were still working full-time. Is that more or less it?"

Megan answered for them, "Yes, that's right. We want to have enough income in retirement to be able to live as well as we did before retirement. Can you tell us how to make that happen?"

"I'll try," said Jim. "It would help a lot, of course, if I knew how the world was going to unfold. Some things are relatively easy to predict, like your retirement income needs. Other parts of the picture are a little fuzzier, like the investment returns you can expect on your retirement savings. The capital markets have a tendency to surprise."

"Is there any way to avoid those surprises?" asked Megan.

"Not if you plan on taking some risks with your investments, and really, you have no choice if you want to get the returns you'll need. The good news is that we are not going into this exercise totally blind. We do know how investments have performed in the past, and that gives us at least an inkling of what we might expect going forward."

"Just an inkling?" asked Megan.

"Well, maybe more than that, but only if we can identify the forces driving the capital markets and then determine how they're changing."

Brett observed, "That sounds like a tall order."

"It's not trivial," Jim conceded, "but I know you're up to the task. We just need to take it step by step. Let's first consider the historic performance of investment returns and inflation and see what they can teach us. I have all the necessary statistics going back to 1938. We will break that long period down into overlapping 30-year periods, since 30 years is how long you intend to save.

"The first 30-year period for which we have data runs from 1938 to 1967, the second from 1939 to 1968 and so on, up to 1990 to 2019. In total, there are 53 overlapping 30-year periods."

"How would that data be useful?" Brett challenged. "I would think that every period tells a different story."

"Or rather, that every period provides a different aspect of the same big story," Jim offered. "When you put them all together, they can give you an idea of how safe you should feel saving a certain fixed percent of pay every year."

Brett wondered aloud, "But which 'fixed percentage'? Isn't that what we're trying to figure out?"

"We'll start with a best guess, which we can modify later, after we see the results it produces. From previous work I've done, I know that saving 10 percent of pay would have been enough at some points in the past, but this is the 21st century and, so far, it has not been kind to savers and retirees. Interest rates are a lot lower than they used to be. Saving 10 percent of pay will almost certainly not be enough; not if you're retiring at 63 and not if you encounter any nasty surprises along the way."

"What do the big pension plans contribute?" asked Megan.

"Do you mean the public sector plans?" asked Jim. "If you combine employee and employer contributions, it is a little over 20 percent of pay."

"Wow! But you're saying we don't need to save that much?"

"I don't think you do," Jim replied. "Those plans have different goals, which aren't especially relevant to your situation, but we'll leave that particular discussion for another day. For now, let's start with a 12 percent saving rate and see where that takes you.

"We will use the worst of the 53 historic periods and show how you would have fared had you lived through it, saving 12 percent a year for the entire time. If you can weather that particular storm, it should give you some confidence that you can handle whatever the future has in store."

Brett and Megan perked up. This sounded like it might almost be fun, at least using the low actuarial bar for what constitutes fun. Brett had a question, "How do you define 'worst'?"

"There are different ways of defining it," Jim acknowledged. "Let's go with the period that produced the lowest real return."

Jim noticed a flicker of uncertainty in their eyes and explained, "When I say 'real returns,' I mean the returns over and above inflation. For instance, the average *nominal* return on a given portfolio over the entire 82 years ending in 2019 happens to be 8.7 percent, while inflation averaged 3.6 percent. That means the average real return was 4.9 percent."[1]

"Why are we looking at real returns?" asked Megan.

"Because they are more meaningful than nominal returns. Inflation tends to mask what is really going on. If you invest in a GIC that earns a 1 percent nominal return, you might think you're growing your wealth; but if inflation is 2 percent, you're actually falling further behind with every passing day. Taking inflation out of the equation enables us to see your true financial situation more clearly.

"There is another reason to focus on real returns. In some of our projections, we are going to churn out some really big numbers. Unadjusted, they might not make much sense because they are based on high historic inflation rates. We will be stripping inflation out of them to produce numbers that we can better relate to."

---

[1] The perceptive reader might think this is a mistake, since simple subtraction yields 5.1 percent. The proper way to determine the real return in this case is to divide 1.087 by 1.036. That produces 1.049.

Brett had already moved on, "What was the worst 30-year period according to your definition?"

"That would be the one that ran from 1946 to the end of 1975. The end point is the year after the worst bear market since the Great Depression. It's not generally known, but the 1973–74 bear market produced bigger investment losses than the global financial meltdown of 2008–09."

"What exactly is a bear market?" asked Megan.

"It's defined as a drop of at least 20 percent in a benchmark index like the S&P/TSX."

"Sounds nasty. Do these bear markets occur frequently?"

"There have been at least eight of them since 1950," Jim confirmed. "That is why there are so many years when overall stock returns have been negative."

"Is the 1973–74 bear market the reason that 1946 to 1975 turned out to be the worst-ever period?" Brett asked.

"It's one reason. Another is that inflation started rising in the mid-1960s and was still climbing by 1975. It caused interest rates to rise, which created losses in the bond portion of one's portfolio."

"Just how bad was 1946 to 1975?"

Jim briefly consulted his chart and noted, "The average real return in that period was 2.6 percent a year, compounded."

"So, even in the worst-ever 30-year period, our investments would still be beating inflation by 2.6 percent a year," said Megan thoughtfully. "That doesn't sound so bad."

"For sure," Jim agreed as he pulled a piece of paper out of his folder. "This graph shows the average return over all 30-year periods, both in nominal and in real terms."

Brett stared at the page and frowned, "Doesn't the return depend on how you invest?"

"Absolutely," said Jim. "I should have mentioned earlier that I'm assuming a 60-40 asset mix."

Jim noticed Brett and Megan exchanging glances, so he added, "A 60-40 asset mix means 60 percent of the assets are invested in stocks (or at least in some pooled or mutual fund that is composed of stocks) while the other 40 percent is invested in bonds, in this case longer-term Government of Canada bonds."

Figure 1: Average returns on a 60-40 asset mix

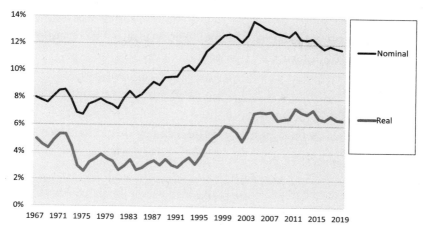

Over 30-year period ending in year shown

While his audience digested that information, Jim continued, "I'm not saying that 60-40 is the ideal asset mix for you, but it is pretty standard for pension funds and retirement saving in general. Later we'll try to improve on it, but for now, let's assume that your savings are invested in a 60-40 mix. Now I need to ask you two, how much are you currently earning?"

Brett hesitated a moment, "I have no problem in giving you that information, Jim, since you're like our financial priest. But why is it important to know our earnings? Don't people need to save the same percentage of pay whether they're earning $25,000 or $250,000?"

"Actually, no," Jim replied. "It is important to include your pensions from OAS and CPP to really understand your retirement-readiness. When you do that, you find that the higher your earnings, the more you might have to save in percentage terms, since OAS and CPP become less and less important to your overall financial well-being."

Brett let that sink in before responding, "Well, we're earning about $110,000 a year between the two of us. And we both can expect to get promoted a few years from now."

"Excellent," said Jim. "Now, here is what I'm going to do in my spreadsheet:

- Input your starting salaries.
- Project them year by year into the future, increasing them by both the national average of wage inflation from 1946 to 1975 and also by my estimate of the additional salary increases you will both earn due to promotions and merit.
- Each year, deduct 12 percent from your combined pay and assume it is invested in a 60-40 asset mix, where both the stock and bond portions of the portfolio earn the actual returns that would have been earned during the period 1946 to 1975."

Megan wondered aloud, "I guess it's like we will be living through the investment and inflation scenario that existed between 1946 and 1975, but with our current salaries as opposed to historical pay."

"That's right," Jim confirmed. "Since I already set up the spreadsheet, it won't take long to do the calculation."

Jim opened up his laptop, clicked away for a couple of minutes on the keyboard and then announced, "I have your answer."

Brett and Megan sucked in their breath.

"After 30 years of saving under these conditions, you would have an account balance of $2,742,000."

A few seconds passed before they could register what Jim had told them. The number was literally beyond anything they could have imagined. Brett spoke first, "That sounds incredible. You're saying if we relive the worst-ever 30-year period saving 12 percent a year, we'll have millions."

Jim said, "Yes, but it comes with a caveat. This figure represents your account balance in *nominal* terms 30 years from now. In other words, it includes 30 years of inflation, which in that era was rather high. Over the years from 1946 to 1975, CPI (price inflation) increased by 229 percent, which means prices at the end of the period would have more than tripled."

"Tripled?" Brett questioned. "You mean doubled, don't you?"

"No, I mean tripled, because if prices rise by 229 percent, it means they are 329 percent as much as they were at the start. You have to add the original 100 percent back in."

Megan stared out the window as she tried to form her thoughts. "Are you saying we'll be millionaires in 30 years, but it won't be enough because we'll be paying $50 for a loaf of bread?"

"Well, not quite $50, but you get the general idea," said Jim. "I do admit that a number like $2.7 million means nothing until we put it into context. The next step is to convert that lump sum into an income stream. But it's getting late. Can we leave that analysis until the next time we meet?"

"You mean we won't be finishing today?" asked Megan, looking a little disappointed.

"I'm afraid this process we've embarked on will take a while, if you want to do it right. This seems as good a place to break as any."

"Of course," Megan responded, "but you should know we're not going to be able to sleep until we know what happens with our $2.7 million. Are you free tomorrow?"

"I think so," Jim replied. "I'll check my calendar at home and text you with a time. Next time we'll meet at my place, since it'll be easier to access data we might need going forward. But before I go, let me try to summarize where we stand:

- The future may be a mystery, but knowing you could have saved 12 percent and survived the worst 30-year investment period in history should give you some comfort.
- For investing purposes, the worst 30-year period (in real terms) since 1938 ran from 1946 to 1975.
- If you saved 12 percent a year for the next 30 years and experienced the same inflation and investment returns as prevailed between 1946 and 1975, you would accumulate $2,742,000 after 30 years."

Jim wrapped it up with an observation: "We still don't know what that big number means, but stay tuned."

After Jim left, Brett and Megan remained subdued until dinner time as they both thought about what Jim had told them. Brett secretly wondered if they'd still be selling bread in loaves in 30 years.

A bit more about . . . Jim's Projection of Assets

Jim used a 60-40 asset mix, in which 30 percent was invested in Canadian common stocks (original source TSX), 30 percent in US common stocks (source Standard & Poor's) and 40 percent in Canada long bonds. All data came from the publication 2019 *Canadian Economic Statistics* by the Canadian Institute of Actuaries. Securities were assumed to be purchased on December 31 of the previous year and sold on December 31 of the current year. US common stocks are converted to Canadian dollars, and the return includes the gain or loss on the currency. Returns also include applicable dividends, interest and coupon payments plus any capital gain or loss. No transaction costs are assumed. The assets are assumed to be rebalanced each December 31 to maintain the 60-40 asset mix.

Salaries are assumed to rise by the average industrial wage in Canada plus a component for merit increases of 4 percent per annum for the first 10 years, 2 percent for the next 10 years and 0 percent for the subsequent five years. In their final five years of work, Brett's and Megan's salaries are assumed to increase in line with CPI. The asset management fee assumed is 60 basis points per annum. Starting salaries for Jim and Megan combined totalled $110,000.

CHAPTER 3

Converting a Lump Sum into Annual Income

Sunday, May 30

They agreed to meet at 4 p.m. the next day at Jim's place. Jim had set up some lawn chairs in the backyard. After everyone had settled in with a drink, Jim got down to business.

"When we concluded yesterday, I said that if you save 12 percent and relive the period between 1946 and 1975, your savings would grow to about $2.7 million. I can't guarantee you'll actually reach this figure in 30 years' time, but that's not your goal in any case."

"It's not?" asked Brett.

"No, what you really want to know is how much income your savings can produce. If we find that the worst-ever period in modern history could have provided enough income to meet your needs, it should boost your confidence in your future prospects."

"Right, so what happens next?"

"Next, we'll determine how much lifetime income you could expect from all sources, given $2.7 million in savings," Jim replied.

"All sources?" echoed Megan. "What else is there besides our savings?"

"You will also get a pension from OAS and CPP."

Brett made a face. "Is it really a good idea to include government pensions for planning purposes?"

"It is imperative," said Jim, "because OAS and CPP will form a significant part of your overall retirement income. Remember, we are trying to determine whether you can retire comfortably, and answering that question requires that you take all sources of income into account."

Brett persisted, "But what if OAS and CPP aren't there for us when we retire?"

"There is no reason to think that will be the case," said Jim. "The last major changes to OAS pensions took place in the early 1970s. While a clawback was introduced later on, I doubt it is going to affect you."

"What's a clawback?" asked Megan.

"It's when the government gives you something and then takes it away. In this case, the government makes you pay back some or all of your OAS pension if they think you have too much income after age 65. The clawback is like a special tax equal to 15 percent of your income over a certain threshold that changes year by year. That threshold was $79,054 in 2020. If your income gets high enough, the entire OAS pension would be clawed back."

"That doesn't sound like a good thing," Megan offered.

Jim reassured them, "The clawback threshold is indexed to the inflation rate and is applied on an individual basis, not as a couple. Based on my calculations, it will be higher than your projected retirement income, so I don't think you need to worry about it.

"What you do need to worry about more is a change in the starting age for OAS pensions. It might be delayed to age 67 at some point, instead of the current 65. Years ago, the Harper government announced it was going to push it back to 67, but Trudeau rolled it back to 65 when he took office in 2015. Still, I think it is just a matter of time before the starting age is changed, because people are living longer and the government wants most of us to work longer. Note that a similar change has been made to the Social Security systems of almost every other developed country. Still, I wouldn't worry about it. You might be grandfathered in, and even if you're not, that one change is relatively small and would barely affect the calculations."

"Does the CPP pension get clawed back too?" asked Megan.

"No, it doesn't, and there is a very good reason why it never will be. Whereas OAS is totally funded from the government's general revenues, all the money contributed to the CPP comes from workers and their employers. The government doesn't fund it at all, so it doesn't make sense for them to poke their noses in and confiscate any of the benefit."

Brett and Megan looked a little skeptical, so Jim continued, "I get it, the government can poke its nose wherever it wants, but think of it this way: the CPP has been around for over half a century and there has never been any hint that the government might cut benefits.[1] Now, if it turns out that there isn't enough money in the CPP fund to pay full benefits, then yes, CPP pensions could in theory be reduced. What is far more likely, though, is that the level of benefit will be left untouched and active workers and their employers will simply be forced to contribute more. Since this wouldn't affect my income projections, we can proceed to the next step. I'm going to estimate how much CPP and OAS pension would be payable in 30 years' time if you experienced the same inflation as occurred between 1946 and 1975."

Brett interjected, "But wait, there was no CPP or OAS in 1946!"

"No, there wasn't," confirmed Jim, "but remember we are using modern salaries and modern government pension programs and projecting them ahead. This is a simulation into the future using historic assumptions for investment returns and inflation. It makes sense to assume the current pension programs exist throughout the simulation because that is the most likely situation.

"Once I've estimated future CPP and OAS pensions, I'm going to optimize your retirement income using the principles set out in the book *Retirement Income for Life: Getting More without Saving More.*"

"What do you mean when you say 'optimize'?" asked Megan.

"When the time comes, you will be able to choose when you start your CPP pension. The permitted starting age ranges from age 60 to age 70. Usually, you can maximize the amount of lifetime pension by deferring CPP pension to age 70. That is what I am showing in Figure 2. The matter

---

1   Jim is glossing over the change in the pension calculation from the use of three-year average earnings to a five-year average. This happened in the 1980s with no fanfare and little public reaction.

of optimizing your income is an exercise that includes picking the best starting age for CPP. Decumulation is a book in itself, so I'm not going to go into it now; you'll have to trust me on this.

"Consider this chart. It is an example of how retirement income could be optimized for a couple who was retiring now and had $600,000 in RRSP assets. As you can see, the amount of income from CPP and OAS combined (the green bars) is more than half the total income this couple can expect. That's why we can't ignore government pensions. In the future, CPP will be even more important, since the program is in the process of expanding, but it will take decades to phase in."[2]

Figure 2: The importance of CPP and OAS

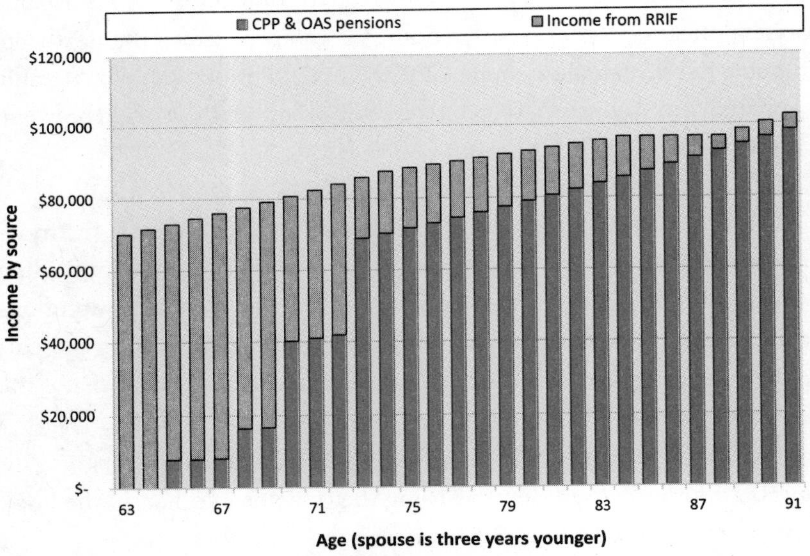

Age (spouse is three years younger)

A couple retiring now with $600,000 in an RRSP. CPP and OAS income dominates. (CPP is deferred to age 70.) This assumes median future returns and 2% annual inflation.

"I see your point," said Brett.

"I did the optimization before you came today," Jim continued. "The result is that you could expect income from all sources in your first year of retirement to be $349,000."

---

2   More on this in Appendix A.

Once again, Brett and Megan were shocked into silence. Finally, Megan spoke, "That is hardly believable, Jim. It's three times as much as we're making right now working full-time."

Jim replied, "Let me remind you that this calculation includes 30 years' worth of inflation from a time when inflation was rather high. Consumer prices more than tripled over the 30 years ending in 1975, and that is baked into our projection. To make sense out of such an inflated figure, we need to compare it to pay that is similarly inflated. To be more precise, we should divide that projected income figure by your average gross pay in the last five years before retirement."

"And when you do that, what does that give you?"

"I get 42 percent."

Yet again, Brett and Megan were left speechless. Megan wanted to make sure she understood right: "You're telling me that even with $2.7 million in savings we'll only be able to produce income equal to 42 percent of our final pay? I guess we won't be travelling to Europe after we retire."

Brett chimed in, "Forget Europe. Even Buffalo looks to be out of the picture."

"I realize it doesn't sound good," Jim conceded, "but it isn't nearly as bad as you think."

"Have you ever been to Buffalo?" Brett asked.

"I mean your retirement income isn't as bad as you think!" Jim clarified. "In fact, we can get you to the right figure without too much work and with no hardship on your part."

"What did you put in that drink, Jim?" asked Brett. "How can you say 42 percent is okay, or almost okay? I read somewhere that our retirement income target should be 70 percent of final pay," said Brett.

A half-smile came across Jim's face, which he immediately tried to suppress. "We need to come to a better understanding of your retirement income target; but for today, all you need to know is that it's not 70 percent. Once we do calculate your real target, I'm going to show you that you can survive even a worst-case scenario like 1946 to 1975."

Brett and Megan looked at each other in silence. They were clearly wondering if it had been a good idea to seek Jim's help.

"So, you're going to turn this into a cliff-hanger?" Megan asked with a frown.

"Surely that's enough pension talk for one day!" Jim declared. "Think of this exercise as a marathon, not a sprint. Since it will take a while, it might be wise to block off a specific day and time every week. That will make it easier to schedule these sessions and give me time to do a little research. Just pick a time that's good for you."

They all liked the idea of Saturdays at 4 p.m. and blocked that time off on their calendars for the next month. Little did they realize that these sessions would last all summer.

Brett and Megan thanked Jim for his time and trouble. As they were about to leave Jim's backyard and make their way home, Megan turned around one last time and implored Jim, "Please tell us it's going to be okay."

After the briefest hesitation, Jim said, "It's going to be okay."

A bit more about . . . How Jim Calculated Income of 42 percent of Final Average Pay

Jim took the accumulation of $2.7 million and fed it into an Excel spreadsheet that is a special version of PERC.[3] This version estimated projected CPP and OAS pensions for Brett and Megan and also determined that their best strategy was to defer CPP to age 68 (they wouldn't have quite enough money in their RRSP or RRIF to defer CPP all the way to age 70 and still produce the income curve they wanted later in life). Under that projection, they would still receive OAS at 65. This optimization process was used to determine retirement income because it produced more income than assuming CPP started immediately upon retirement. It was assumed they would be paying investment management fees of 0.6 percent a year. On this basis, Excel projected their combined income in 30 years' time to be $349,000 from all sources, which translates into 42 percent of their final average five years' earnings before retirement. Also reflected in the calculation was an annual increase in retirement income to match inflation up to age 70, and then smaller increases in subsequent years.

---

3   PERC is a retirement calculator that is described later on.

CHAPTER 4

A Realistic Retirement Income Target

Saturday, June 5

In spite of Jim's assurances, Megan continued to feel troubled about their retirement situation for the rest of the day. She knew how silly that sounded, since she was only 30, but where would the money come from if they had to save more than 12 percent a year? Even saving 12 percent would be a challenge with the mortgage payments they were making. And if they had children . . .

Had Jim known what Megan was going through, he would have held the next session sooner. But the days did eventually pass, and at 4 p.m. the following Saturday, Brett and Megan made their way to Jim's place. He wasn't answering the front doorbell, so they peeked into the open garage. When they saw Jim there, retirement income targets seemed to be the furthest thing from his mind. He was holding a few pieces of hardware in his hand and looking baffled.

Jim looked up blankly and asked, "Is it four o'clock already? Sorry, I got side-tracked trying to fix this old lawnmower. I should really get a new one." He put the pieces down and led his neighbours into the house instead of the backyard. He explained, "We're going to have to use the computer and printer this time, so it's better if we meet in my living room where I've set everything up."

Jim showed them into the living room while he went to wash his hands. When he returned, Megan was staring at a framed black-and-white photo of a young girl that she had spied on the mantelpiece. "Is that your grand-daughter?" she asked.

Even before Jim answered, Megan realized her mistake. The photo was obviously dated. Megan also noticed there were no photos anywhere of Jim's wife.

Jim answered without emotion, "That's my daughter." And then almost as if he were speaking to himself, he added, "She'd be about your age now."

Megan sensed it was best not to ask any more questions.

Once they were sitting down, Jim got right down to business, "I know you weren't happy with the results I calculated last time. I showed that saving 12 percent a year would produce retirement income equal to just 42 percent of final pay. I know that didn't sound like a lot, especially since it included CPP and OAS. You might take some consolation in the fact that this result happened under the worst investment conditions since they started keeping records,[1] but then again, I can't promise you the future will be any better. What I want to show you today is that having retirement income equal to 42 percent of your final average pay isn't all that bad."

"We always assumed we might have to be a little more careful with money after retirement," said Megan, "but 42 percent? It sounds like it will involve a lot of belt-tightening."

"Actually, no," Jim assured her, "although it will take a little while to show you why."

"It's hard not to be skeptical," Brett admitted and gave Megan a squeeze of the shoulder.

Jim explained, "Here is what we're going to do. We will drill deeper into how you spend your money, both now and in the future. It is critically important to understand this if we are going to determine how much you

---

1   1946 to 1975

have to save. If you don't mind, then, I'd like to ask you some questions about your long-term spending plans."

Glancing over at Megan, Brett said, "Sounds good, Jim. Fire away."

Over the course of the next half hour, Jim asked a series of questions and made notes as Brett and Megan replied. He continued to write for a few more minutes while the young couple looked on in silence.

Eventually, Jim looked up and announced, "We're done! I have listed the major spending categories during your working years. Let me know if this sounds about right to you."

Jim showed them a handwritten chart.

Table 1: Spending highlights during the working years

In your 30s	Mortgage payments on a starter home, costs for daycare and after-school care, purchase of durables like furniture and appliances
In your 40s	Trading up to a larger home with bigger mortgage payments, purchase of more durables
In your early to mid-50s	Mortgage payments taper off as a percentage of pay, the children's university costs ramp up
In your late 50s and early 60s	Mortgage is finally paid off, child-related expenses diminish, maybe a reno
In all periods	Saving for retirement, mortgage payments and job-related costs

Brett and Megan reviewed the list and nodded slowly. "Yup, that about sums it up," said Brett.

Jim continued, "Just give me an hour to feed this data into my spreadsheet. See you maybe at five o'clock?"

When Brett and Megan returned, paper was scattered everywhere in Jim's living room.

"Well, someone's been busy," noted Megan.

"I took the spending summary we mapped out and used it as a guide to create a detailed breakdown of your spending over the next 30 years. The major categories I've created are:

- mortgage payments,
- child-raising expenses,
- work-related expenses,
- saving for retirement,
- income tax and
- everything else (what we will call 'spendable income').

"We'll start with the mortgage payments. You told me that you took out a five-year closed, fixed mortgage, so payments will change every five years when you renew." With that, Jim handed out a sheet to summarize.

Table 2: Annual mortgage payments

Ages (Brett)	Annual amount	Average % of pay
33–37	$27,500	20%
38–42	$26,793	11%
43–47	$77,217	22%
48–52	$91,461	18%
53–57	$89,425	14%
58–62	$96,019	12%

Brett noted, "Well, I recognize the first number, $27,500. We are paying nearly $2,300 a month toward the mortgage. When we took out the mortgage last year, the payments were exactly 25 percent of our combined gross pay, which was the most I figured we could afford. But I see you're showing that it averages out to just 20 percent of pay over the first five years instead of 25 percent."

"That's because the mortgage payments are level in dollar terms while your pay is rising," explained Jim. "Remember, we're using the economic scenario from 1946 to 1975 when it comes to investment returns and inflation. To be consistent, we also have to use the pay increases that would have been appropriate in that era. Back then, wages were rising quite a bit faster than price inflation."

"Why do the mortgage payments in dollar terms dip slightly between ages 38 and 43?" Brett asked.

"I didn't think that was going to be your main question about the table," Jim noted, "but I can explain that easily. In the early years of the 1946–75 period, interest rates fell, which lowered mortgage payments. The lower mortgage payments between ages 38 to 43 reflect that. Remember you need to renegotiate your payments every five years."

"I see the mortgage payments nearly triple by age 43," said Megan, with some concern in her voice. "What is going on there?"

"Ah, that is what I thought you were going to ask first!" Jim exclaimed. "You mentioned your plan to buy a larger home eventually, so I made the assumption that you would be trading up when Brett is 43 and you're 40. At that point, I am assuming you would buy a new home equal to the equity you built up in your current home plus whatever size of mortgage results in payments of 25 percent of pay."

Brett thought about that for a moment and nodded. "That sounds reasonable. And you kept on changing the mortgage rates throughout the 30 years?"

"Yes, because I tried to make this scenario as realistic as possible. Every five years when you have to renegotiate your mortgage, I am reflecting the interest rates that prevail at that time, and in general, rates were rising in the latter half of the 1946–75 period."

"Okay," Brett conceded, "I can go along with that, although it's a little difficult to wrap my head around the salary increases and interest rates from that era. What do we do with this information?"

"For now, you park it," said Jim. "Let's move on to child-raising costs. This time, the costs do vary year by year, but I've simplified the results by presenting them in five-year groupings."

And with that, Jim handed out another piece of paper.

Table 3: Child-raising costs

Ages (Brett)	Annual average	Average % of pay
33–37	$25,973	17%
38–43	$42,244	18%
43–47	$42,562	12%
48–52	$68,580	15%
53–57	$65,049	10%
58–62	$33,491	4%

It was Megan's turn to jump in with a question. "When are you assuming we start having children?" she asked coyly.

"I am assuming in the second year of the projection, which would be next year, of course. You did tell me you plan to start a family soon."

"I see," said Megan, "but why are the child costs so high in the first 10 years?

"Actually, they could easily have been higher than what I'm showing," Jim replied. "To determine child-related costs, I used a spreadsheet I found online. It was developed by Ernst & Young, one of the big four accounting firms,[2] and I found it to be quite thorough. For each possible cost item, their spreadsheet allows a range of costs — low, medium and high — or you can input a custom amount. The costs would have been much lower in the early years if it weren't for daycare followed by after-school child care, but I'm assuming you stay fully employed during those years."

"Still, I'm surprised by some of the numbers. I wouldn't mind seeing a breakdown," Megan declared.

"And so, you shall," Jim assured her.[3]

Casting a sidelong glance at Brett, Megan noted, "If one of us stays home for a few years, we could avoid the daycare costs."

"Yes," said Jim, nodding, "but then you would be missing one whole salary, and I don't think you'd like how the numbers would play out under that scenario."

---

2   You can access this by googling "Cost of Raising a Child Calculator — TMOAP Official Version."

3   It is shown at the end of this chapter.

Megan persisted, "Fair enough. Work it is for both of us, then. But you must have been using E&Y's high estimate in each year for the numbers to be so high."

"No, for the most part, I used their medium assumptions. Even the midpoint of the range of daycare costs is expensive. Moreover, I made no allowance for vacations before the children were 10, or even for summer camps. I did assume, however, that you and Brett would help pay for university tuition and lodging. Overall, I would say my estimates are a little on the low side."

"Why do the child costs continue until the last five years of the projection?" asked Brett. "Shouldn't these kids you invented be out of the house by then?"

"Once again, I'm trying to be realistic. By that point your children would be around age 25, and while they might have jobs and be more or less self-supporting (fingers crossed), it is not at all unusual for parents to continue to provide some financial help, say, by continuing to pay cell phone bills or subsidizing the rent or picking up the bill when you go to restaurants together. Even though the dollar costs look high in the table for those last five years, they represent just 4 percent of your pay."

Brett and Megan continued to stare at the chart, mesmerized.

"All the percentages I'm showing for child costs could easily have been several percentage points higher," Jim continued. "Actually, the child costs *were* a little higher than shown, but I applied the Canada child benefit (CCB) as an offset."

Jim paused. "I've been asking you to absorb a lot of numerical information today, which I know can't be easy. The good news is that the hard part is done. I'll be able to get through the other expenses much more quickly. This next table shows the final three categories of spending that whittle down your paycheques."

Table 4: Other pre-retirement costs

Ages (Brett)	Work-related	Income tax	Retirement saving
33–37	10%	18%	12%
38–43	9%	19%	12%
43–47	8%	20%	12%
48–52	7%	21%	12%
53–57	7%	22%	12%
58–62	6%	23%	12%

Megan asked, "I see the work-related expenses start at 10 percent in the early years. Why are they so high?"

"I've included contributions to CPP and EI as well as any provincial health premium you might be paying. I also make some allowance for commuting to work, paying for business meals and business attire you might have to buy. If anything, 10 percent might be low . . ."

"Why do work-related expenses go down in later years?" Megan persisted.

Jim explained, "Your contributions to CPP and EI are capped at a certain dollar threshold, so the higher your earnings rise above that threshold, the less you're paying as a percentage of pay."

Switching gears, Brett asked, "How did you calculate income tax?"

"I assumed the current tax rates would continue to apply in future years and that all the dollar limits on tax brackets and credits would be indexed to inflation. I also assumed you would get a tax deduction for the 12 percent that you're saving toward retirement. That implies you're putting the money into an RRSP."

Next, Jim handed out a new chart. "Now it's time to bring it all together. I've input all these percentages to create a graph.

"When you subtract retirement saving, work-related expenses, child-raising costs, mortgage payments and income tax, it leaves you with what I call 'spendable income.' This term is a catch-all that includes spending on food, clothing, entertainment, utilities, insurance premiums, property taxes and pretty much anything else you can think of other than what you spend on your kids."

Figure 3: Breaking down pay (when saving 12%)

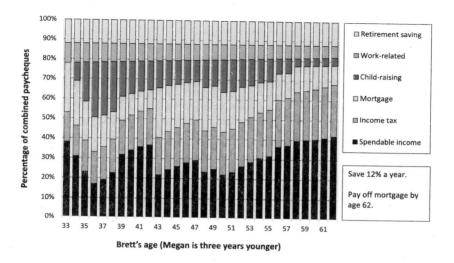

Brett's age (Megan is three years younger)

"The ones we don't have," Megan pointed out.

"Yet."

"Am I reading this right?" asked Brett. "The most we ever spend on ourselves is just 42 percent of pay?"

"Yes, that would be your spendable income in the year before you retire. It's more appropriate to take the average over the last five years, which would lower it to 41 percent."

"I wouldn't have believed our spendable income could be so low if you hadn't shown me the spending breakdown line by line," Brett mused. "I still feel I'm missing something, but I don't know what."

While Brett pondered that question, Megan jumped in: "And you're saying that we don't need more retirement income to cover the other spending categories?"

"If you play your cards right, all the spending categories should disappear by the time you retire, except for 'spendable income' and 'income tax.' Your children should be self-supporting, your mortgage should be paid and you would no longer be saving for retirement. If you wanted to have enough income to match your spendable income in the last five years of work, at least the way it is shown on this chart, that would be 41 percent of your final average pay plus the amount you have to pay in income tax."

Brett studied the chart intently. "If we add in income tax, which is over 20 percent on the chart, it looks like the income target should be over 60 percent."

"Actually, it will be a lot less than that, since you will be paying much less income tax in retirement, both in dollar terms and percentage terms. Without doing a precise calculation, I would estimate the total spending target, including tax, to be just about 50 percent."

"How do you get 50 percent?" Brett asked.

"At this income level, income tax in retirement would be slightly less than 20 percent of total income," Jim clarified, "so if you add 20 percent of 41 percent, it brings you up to about 50 percent of gross pay. But even 50 percent isn't the right number."

"It's not?"

"No, because we'll be adjusting your mortgage payments and saving rate before we're done, and when we do, the percentage of income you need will come down a little more. The important point for today is that you should no longer worry about trying to generate retirement income of 70 percent of final average pay, or even 60 percent."

Brett and Megan started to relax for the first time that day. Still, Brett wasn't quite ready to throw in the towel. "Then why are all the public-sector pension plans based on a retirement income target of 70 percent? Is there something you're not telling us?"

After a long pause, Jim said, "It's complicated. Thirty years ago, the federal government felt they had to defend the high public sector pensions. The minister of finance at the time stated publicly that public sector workers had lower salaries than their counterparts in the private sector, and that this justified higher pensions for the public sector. But then public sector wages caught up and that rationale no longer worked."

"Did they reduce pension levels in the public sector when that happened?" asked Brett.

"No, they just changed the rationale for the higher pensions. Nowadays, the most common defence of high pensions is that not every civil servant retires with 35 years of pensionable service, so the average pension actually received isn't excessive after all."

"But if one works for a shorter period, shouldn't pensions be proportionately less?" Brett asked.

Unknowingly, Brett had struck a sore point.

"You would think," exclaimed Jim. "The defenders of big pensions seem to have glossed over that point."

"What you're saying is that governments are using bogus arguments to justify a 70 percent target," Brett declared, more as a statement than a question.

"Actually, the situation is even worse than that," said Jim. "When you include OAS pensions plus the recent enhancement in CPP pensions, the target is closer to 80 percent pension after 35 years of service. As we have just seen, this is far more than anyone needs to maintain their standard of living after retirement."

Brett and Megan just shook their heads in disbelief. This time, Megan spoke up. "Why doesn't someone do something about this?"

"Who do you suggest?" asked Jim. "Most newspaper journalists don't really understand this, and besides, they know that 20 percent of their paid readership work in the public sector. It may not be in the interests of the newspapers to be seen to attack them. Senior management within the public sector could say something, but they participate in these very same pension plans, so they'd be arguing against their own self-interest."

"What about politicians?" Megan asked. "The people we elect to serve us?"

"It's especially hard for them to say anything," Jim replied. "First, they have divided loyalties, as the staff that they interact with on a daily basis participate in these plans. It would make for some awkward internal meetings if the MPs were to start making public declarations that these pensions are too rich. Second, politicians are not keen to alienate the public sector unions, either. Third, they don't want to call attention to their own pensions, which are even more generous!"

"Well, what about actuaries like you, Jim?" asked Megan. "You guys understand what's going on. You could speak up!"

Jim shook his head. "Pension actuaries certainly understand the issues, but much of their business comes from the public sector, so their hands are tied. No one in a major actuarial firm is willing to speak publicly against the interests of their clients."

Brett and Megan had nothing left to say.

After a brief pause, Jim continued, "I don't want to end this session on a negative note. The important takeaway, as far as you're concerned, is that your retirement income target is a lot more attainable than you thought. We have established that your target is roughly 50 percent of final average pay, or maybe a tad less. Just as I promised, the 42 percent of income we calculated under that worst-case scenario is not that far off."

"Thanks, Jim," said Megan. "That's a relief. Thanks also for your insights into retirement income targets in general. I feel as if we've been let in on a big secret."

Brett wasn't prepared to be quite so generous, "I agree that 42 percent doesn't sound so bad now, but it still leaves us short of our 50 percent target."

"I hear you, Brett," said Jim. "And believe me, we will close that gap before we're through. But we won't be doing it today. Right now, I have to fix my lawn mower."

A bit more about . . . The Cost of Raising a Child

The table below shows some of the costs of raising a child that Jim used in his calculations. Costs per child are shown for four sample ages. Inflationary increases for later years are not reflected here.

	Age 1	Age 7	Age 13	Age 20
Housing	$1,200	$1,200	$1,200	$1,200
Food	$2,300	$2,300	$2,300	$2,300
Transportation	$1,970	$1,970	$1,970	$1,970
Diapers	$720	Nil	Nil	Nil
Clothing	$737	$737	$737	$737
Health care	$1,207	$1,207	$1,207	Nil
Full-time or after-school child care	$14,400	$4,200	Nil	Nil
Extracurriculars	$2,400	$2,400	$2,400	Nil
Education supplies	$600	$600	$600	Nil
Saving for university	Nil	Nil	Nil	$8,400
Vacations	Nil	Nil	$3,000	$3,000
Cell phone	Nil	Nil	$600	$600

Saving for university starts earlier than when a child is age 20, but this is not shown in the table because it highlights only sample ages. Also, the table doesn't show "help with rent," which started at age 22. Some costs have obviously been smoothed out, since they are shown as being the same at each age. The overall costs could have been higher because the calculations assumed no vacation costs before age 10 and only a nominal amount for more expensive activities like summer camps, organized sports and various lessons. No lost income by either parent was assumed, though some is possible, even with allowance being made for full-time or after-school care.

The sources of information that Ernst & Young used to create this table are as follows:

U.S. Department of Agriculture, *Expenditures on Children by Families*, 2015 annual report

Christopher A. Sarlo, Fraser Institute, "The Cost of Raising Children," August 22, 2013

Mark Brown, *MoneySense*, "The Real Cost of Raising Kids," 2011 and 2015 update

BabyCenter, First-Year Baby Cost Calculator

CHAPTER 5

Should You Pay Off the Mortgage Early?

Sunday, June 6

Brett and Megan heard the dull roar of a lawn mower the next morning as they were having breakfast. Brett waited until the noise stopped before walking over to Jim's place. Jim saw Brett approaching and greeted him with a smile.

"What do you think?" Jim asked, pointing proudly to a shiny new lawn mower.

"I thought you were going to fix the old one," said Brett.

"I've determined that isn't part of an actuary's skill set," Jim replied. "Anyway, it looks like there is something you want to tell me."

Brett spoke excitedly, eager to share his revelation with Jim. "Guess what? I thought of a way that our spendable income in the final five years of work could be a lot higher than the 41 percent you calculated last time."

Jim looked mildly amused. "I'm all ears. Did you want to talk about it now?"

"Well, I don't want to put you out," said Brett, "especially since we did agree to weekly sessions on Saturdays. But if you don't mind, I know Megan happens to be free . . ."

Ten minutes later, they re-assembled on the patio next to Jim's freshly mown lawn. Brett started to explain his revelation, "In your calculations, you showed mortgage payments continuing right up until our retirement date. If we paid off our mortgage sooner, say by the time I'm 57, that would boost our spendable income in our last five years of work by quite a lot, wouldn't it?"

"Yes, it would," Jim agreed.

"And since we now have higher spendable income in our last few years, we would want to raise our retirement income target to match, right?" Brett continued.

"Correct," Jim confirmed.

"Doesn't that mean our target should be close to 70 percent after all?" Brett concluded.

"Nicely argued," Jim replied, "but the math doesn't work. Let me illustrate by using the same projection assumptions as last time. We'll have to go in the house, though, since I'll need the printer."

They re-established themselves in the kitchen while Jim explained, "We will redo the last projection with just one change. The only difference this time is that we'll accelerate your mortgage payments so that the mortgage is fully paid off five years earlier."

Jim tapped away briefly on his laptop, and they soon heard the hum of the printer in the next room. Jim got up to retrieve a sheet of paper from the printer. He returned and started to explain the chart marked Table 5 as he sat back down.

"As in Table 2, I still have you buying your next house at age 43 and making the same, higher mortgage payments for the subsequent five years. Then, at age 48, your mortgage payments suddenly shoot up under the 'Pay off by age 57' scenario. That is because you're amortizing what remains of the mortgage over 10 more years instead of 15."

Table 5: Annual mortgage payments

Ages (Brett)	Pay off by age 62	Pay off by age 57
33–37	$27,500	$27,500
38–43	$26,793	$26,793
43–47	$77,217	$77,217
48–52	$91,461	$119,218
53–57	$89,425	$117,796
58–62	$96,019	Nil

"Comparing these two scenarios, you can see the mortgage payments are higher for 10 years if you pay the mortgage off early, then they drop to zero for the last five years. Let's turn these numbers into percentages of pay and recreate the chart I had labelled as Figure 3. We'll then see what accelerating the mortgage payments does."

Jim made the changes on his computer and printed off yet another chart.

Figure 4: Where the money goes (if mortgage is paid early, percent of pay)

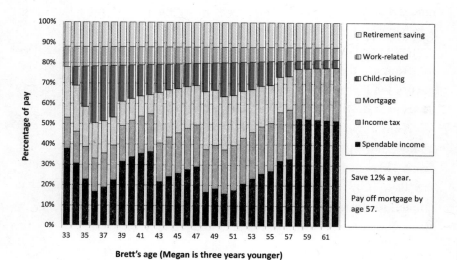

"Here is the result!" Jim announced. "By paying off the mortgage earlier, you've raised your spendable income in the final five years before retirement to 52 percent of final average pay. If we make a rough calculation of the income tax payable in retirement, and add it on top of your regular spending, your retirement income target works out to about 63 percent."

"You see," Brett exclaimed triumphantly, "the target should be 70 percent after all!"

"Not so fast," said Jim. "First of all, 63 percent is not the same as 70 percent. But more importantly, take a closer look at this chart and tell me how much of your income is available for regular spending in the earlier working years."

There was indeed a problem. Brett remained silent just staring at the chart, but Megan chimed in, "Oh my god, it shows our spendable income will be less than 20 percent of pay in our late 40s!"

"That's right," Jim confirmed. "In fact, it was already as low as 17 percent of pay at age 36 with the previous mortgage schedule. Now the problem has just become that much worse. Low spendable income would be something you would have to live with until you're both well into your 50s. For the first 25 years in this chart, your average spendable income would be 24 percent of pay before rising to 52 percent in the last five years.

"Big picture, you only arrive at a retirement income target of over 70 percent by semi-starving yourself until your mid-50s. Or let me put it another way: if you want to persuade me that you need spendable income of 52 percent in retirement, you'd first have to explain why you would be content to live on less than half of that for most of your working lives."[1]

"I see what you mean," said Brett, turning a little red. "It sounds like we shouldn't be trying to pay off the mortgage early."

"Actually, I'm not saying that at all," Jim explained. "I think that paying off your mortgage early is a great idea! We just have to change a few other spending practices to allow you to do that."

"Okay, now you're losing me," said Brett, looking a little frustrated.

Jim attempted to explain. "Until now, we've operated on the basis that the percentages of income you allocate to certain expenses are sacrosanct:

---

[1] Actually, it is just a third of that if Jim showed spendable income in (constant) dollar terms.

specifically, child costs, work-related costs, income tax and retirement saving. When we try to ramp up mortgage payments, your spendable income gets thrown out of whack. It drops much too low in the early stages of your careers and then spikes to an unsustainably high level in the final stage. We can fix this, but it means allowing one of those supposedly untouchable expenses to vary year by year."

"I don't see which one," Brett replied. "We're not going to increase spendable income for Megan and me on the backs of our children, so you can't really reduce child costs. And I don't think my employer or the CRA will let us reduce work-related costs or income tax. So that leaves just retirement saving, but we already fixed it at 12 percent of pay."

"The 12 percent of pay was really just our first stab at how much you'd have to save for retirement," Jim replied. "It was always meant to be a working assumption; a figure we might have to tinker with and not something cast in stone."

Megan declared, "I don't care so much what the number is as long as our standard of living doesn't have to take a step backwards late in our careers, much less in retirement. Once we get used to a certain lifestyle, we aren't going to want to give it up."

"I agree," said Jim. "You want your spendable income to be at a tolerable level in all years and to be rising over time in real terms. In fact, I would argue that this should be the second-most important saving goal. The primary goal is still to save enough by retirement age; but as we're finding out, how you get there is critically important."

Seeing heads nodding, Jim went on, "I admit we seem to be finding more problems than solutions so far, but please be patient. Before we change anything, though, I want to show you one more chart."

Jim then repeated the routine of tapping away on his laptop and walking into the next room to grab something off the printer. He returned and handed the page to Brett and Megan.

"It's pretty!" said Megan. "Did you really do this yourself?"

"We actuaries can be a little OCD when it comes to spreadsheets and graphs," Jim admitted a little sheepishly.

Jim started to explain Figure 5. "You might have a bit of trouble wrapping your mind around this new chart, but it's important that you understand what's going on because we'll be showing similar charts later

Figure 5: Where the money goes (if the mortgage is paid early, constant dollars)

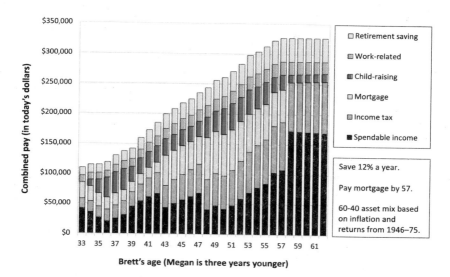

Brett's age (Megan is three years younger)

on. It shows the same thing as the previous chart but now expressed in dollar terms. The hard part is that it's expressed in *today's* dollars, not inflated dollars. I made this conversion by calculating all future amounts and then deflating them by price inflation."

"If it's in current dollars," Brett questioned, "then why does it show our combined pay in 30 years will be nearly triple what it is now?"

"Because that is where I think you will end up after a career of real wage increases," said Jim. "A tripling of pay in real terms over a lifetime is not unusual in salaried positions. Think of an extreme case like a mailroom clerk rising to become CEO. In that case, pay would rise a hundredfold in real terms, if not more."

"And I see there are still no mortgage payments after Brett turns 58," Megan observed.

"Right, because I am recommending that you pay off the mortgage five years before retirement. Brett was right to suggest it. We will assume early liquidation of the mortgage in all our projections from now on."

Brett blushed with the compliment.

"Wouldn't it be more useful if the chart showed our retirement income as well?" Megan questioned.

"Yes, it would," replied Jim, "but I felt the chart was busy enough. This next graph does what you're asking — it shows spendable income, both before and after retirement. I removed everything else from the chart because we agreed that all the other spending items (except income tax) should go away by retirement age. This allows us to focus only on how spendable income changes over time."

Jim handed out a chart showing that spendable income in retirement was barely half as much as in the last five working years.

Figure 6: Spendable income varies widely (if saving 12%)

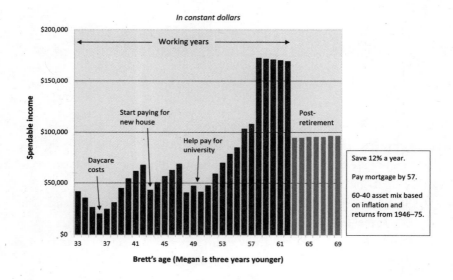

"Great," said Brett with a wink, "now we have graphic proof of just how much hot water we're in."

"That's not the purpose of this chart, but I see why you might think that," said Jim, chuckling. "Doesn't it also give you a hint as to how we can fix the volatility in spendable income?"

"You call this 'volatility'?" said Brett, "I call it 'eating mac and cheese until I die'!"

Megan answered Jim's question more constructively. "Well, it looks like we have a lot more spendable income between ages 58 and 62 than we need, or at least a lot more than we ever had. Maybe we can do something with that?"

"Exactly!" Jim exclaimed. "It's time to make a paradigm change. Your spendable income should not be an afterthought. We are going to make your second goal a reality, which is to smooth out your spendable income over your lifetime, with a nice little upward bias."

"How do we make that happen?" asked Megan.

"I think we should save that until the next time we meet," Jim suggested. "This will take a little time to sort out."

"You're going to leave us hanging again!" exclaimed Megan.

"Only for a little while."

"You know, Jim, we really appreciate what you're doing for us. But it's starting to feel a little like that TV series 24. Just when we resolve one crisis, another one materializes."

"I'm sorry about that," Jim replied, "but I promise this will have a happy ending, unlike that show."

"See you next Saturday, then?" Megan confirmed as they let themselves out.

"If not sooner," Jim replied.

CHAPTER 6

Introducing the Rule of 30

A few days later, Megan and Brett were sitting at home watching TV. Megan was thinking about the photo she had seen in Jim's living room the previous Saturday.

"It's really nice of Jim to be helping us out like this," she said.

"Uh huh," Brett responded as he tried solving the day's Final Jeopardy.

"What do you make of Jim?" she asked.

"I dunno, he's pretty much like any other older guy; except a little smarter, I guess."

"He's that for sure," Megan replied. "It's just that he always seems a little sad."

Brett shrugged his shoulders, and said, "I hope you're not planning to make him one of your projects."

Megan stayed quiet.

The following Saturday when they saw Jim, Megan immediately reminded him of where they had left off. "You know, Jim," she chided, "you left us in suspense the last time we got together. We couldn't seem to get our spendable income at a consistent level, and you promised to tell us how to fix it."

"Yes, well, that's what we're going to work on today," Jim assured her. "The solution lies in changing what is capable of being changed. I sort of hinted last time at what that was."

"Yeah, we got that message alright," Brett responded. "You said the 12 percent saving rate was only a working assumption. I don't see what we can do with it, though. If we save less, it'll boost our spendable income in our working years, but then we aren't saving enough. If we increase it, we might have enough retirement income, but the low spendable income in our working years becomes an even bigger problem."

Jim's eyes lit up. "Nicely summarized, Brett! I see you're really owning this conundrum. I mentioned a paradigm shift, and this is a good time to start talking about it. Until now, you've been thinking in terms of saving a constant percentage of pay throughout your working careers. Obviously, the projections we've been running show that particular approach won't work too well for you. What should you do instead?"

There was silence for a few seconds, then Megan suggested, "Vary our retirement saving percentage?"

"Bingo!" said Jim. "You have almost total flexibility in how much you save for retirement in any given year. You could decide not to save at all until 45, for instance. No one would recommend that, however, because you'd be missing out on the magic of compound interest. Everyone tells you to start saving early, but sometimes that type of advice isn't helpful if it doesn't leave you with enough spendable income to live comfortably. Remember Figure 6 from last time? When Brett is age 36, that chart showed you'd have only $20,000 in spendable income if you tried to save 12 percent of pay that year. That amount would have to cover practically everything you spend money on, other than your children: property taxes, home and car insurance, the cost to run and maintain your car(s), utilities, groceries . . ."

Brett cut him off a little abruptly, "Yes, we get it. It's not a lot."

"I know that some people have no choice but to live on such a small amount because they got the short end of the stick in life, income-wise," Jim continued. "That's unfortunate, and there's not much we can do about it. But in your case, your combined income exceeds $100,000 and will go higher over time. Why would you try to live on $20,000 if you don't have to?

"I want you to get your minds around saving less in lean times and saving more when you're relatively flush with cash. The constant shouldn't be the saving percentage, it should be the degree of difficulty in saving a certain amount each year."

Brett and Megan silently digested Jim's last comment. They both sensed that it could have a major impact on their lives. Jim had more to say on the subject.

"You shouldn't be bullied by retirement experts into saving more than you can afford. I'm sure you've seen articles in the papers that bemoan the woeful lack of retirement saving in this country. The authors seem to have forgotten how hard it can be to save at certain points in one's life cycle. They might believe that young people can and should bear any amount of financial deprivation, but I don't buy it. It would be refreshing to hear what someone age 35 with a middling income, a hefty mortgage and two kids in daycare thinks about that."

"I admit we don't have much left right now at the end of the month, but we can get by," said Megan.

"Good to know, but talk to me again when you have kids in daycare. Saving for retirement will always involve some sacrifice, but there has to be a limit."

Megan had to ask, "What are you suggesting, Jim?"

"That you spread the pain of saving more evenly," said Jim. "This requires you to save more when you can and less when your spendable income is already weighed down by heavier-than-usual expenses."

"I'm all for reducing pain," said Brett, "but how do we know if a particular year is unusually painful, money-wise? Especially when we're in the middle of it?"

"You're not totally in the dark," Jim replied. "Start with mortgage payments. In most cases, the amount that homeowners pay toward their mortgage will vary quite widely over time, as a percentage of pay. Take the 30-year spending projection I put together for you two. In it, your mortgage payments run anywhere from 25 percent of pay down to 9 percent. Making a mortgage payment is more or less the same as putting money into your RRSP. In both cases, you're building up the value of an asset and improving your financial security later in life. To me, it makes perfect sense to combine the two amounts when considering how much to save in a given year."

"How do you mean 'combine'?" asked Megan.

"If you pay more in a given year toward your mortgage, you should feel comfortable contributing less that year into your RRSP. And vice versa."

"Is it just mortgage payments that you would single out for this special treatment?" asked Megan.

"No, not just mortgages, but we have to be very careful about what else we allow as a possible offset because we don't want retirement saving to get crowded out. Saving enough is still the primary goal. That said, I believe an eligible offset could be any expense that has the following characteristics." At this point, Jim looked around the room, as if he were searching for something.

"Jim? Is there something you're looking for?" Megan inquired.

"Just a piece of paper to write on. Ah, here we go." Jim picked up a sheet that had a discarded chart on one side and turned it over to the blank side. He then looked around again for a pen, found one and talked as he wrote.

"As I was saying, to be eligible as an offset against saving for retirement, the expense would have to be:

- extraordinary,
- of relatively short duration (e.g., two or three years),
- unavoidable and
- easily quantifiable.

"Can you think of any expenses that meet these criteria?" Jim asked.

Jim was greeted with silence, so he tried to get them started. "Especially expenses that you're likely to incur sooner rather than later?"

Brett and Megan thought about that for a minute. Brett was thinking backyard pool, but something told him that wasn't the answer Jim was looking for.

It was Megan who spoke first: "Daycare!"

"Very good!" said Jim. "The cost of daycare is significant, lasts a fairly short time and is easily quantifiable. So, yes, we should include it as an offset. "By the way," he added, looking at Brett, "I'm glad you didn't say backyard pool."

Brett stared at Jim in amazement but also managed to look a little wounded.

"Is there anything else you think we should include in the mix?" asked Megan.

"There could be other items, but the shorter we keep the list, the better, for obvious reasons. For now, I propose that you allocate a fixed percentage of your gross income to just those three items: retirement saving, mortgage payments and daycare expenses. The cost of each of those items can be allowed to vary from year to year, but the sum should always be the same. Think of retirement saving as the balancing item."

Brett wanted to make sure he had heard right. "You were serious when you said we wouldn't be saving 12 percent of pay every year for retirement?"

"That's right," Jim confirmed. "Not even 10 percent in some years. And maybe not even 5 percent."

"An actuary telling us that we shouldn't make retirement saving our highest spending priority!" Brett said in an incredulous tone, as if speaking to himself.

"Correct," said Jim. "Saving is not more important than paying for the roof over your heads or for someone to take care of your kids while you work. Moreover, varying your saving percentage ensures you'll have more spendable income when you really need it. Like in your 30s and 40s."

Brett was clearly warming to the idea. "I like it! How much will we save for retirement then?"

"As I said, sometimes it will be more and sometimes less. To show you how this would work, let's look again at the initial projection we made and see how the contributions toward retirement would change. Take a look at this table. You've seen the mortgage costs before; they were included in Table 2. What is new are the daycare expenses. I didn't explicitly show them before because they were buried in the overall child-raising costs."

Table 6: Special expenses and retirement saving (% of pay)

Ages (Brett)	Mortgage payments*	Daycare expenses*	Sum
33–37	20%	7%	27%
38–42	11%	2%	13%
43–47	22%	0%	22%
48–52	22%	0%	22%
53–57	15%	0%	15%
58–62	0%	0%	0%

*Five-year averages

"As you can see," Jim continued, "the percentage of your total pay that you allocate toward the mortgage and daycare is all over the map. This is a major reason why saving is so difficult in some years and fairly easy in others. All we need to do now is set the retirement saving percentage so that the sum of the three spending items equals a certain percentage of pay."

"What percentage would that be?" asked Brett nervously.

"I suggest 30 percent," said Jim.

Brett let that sink in for a moment before asking, "Is there a name for the saving method you're proposing?"

"I don't think so," Jim replied. "Do you think we should give it a name?"

Brett shrugged, but Megan nodded.

"Okay," said Jim. "Let me think."

Jim paced the floor for a few seconds before announcing, "I know, let's call it the 'Rule of 30.'"

"Seriously, Jim, the 'Rule of 30'? I think you've been reading too much Sherlock Holmes," said Megan playfully. "It sounds like *The Sign of Four* or *The Seven-Per-Cent Solution*."

"Oh," said Jim, a little crestfallen.

"But I have to admit, I kind of like it!" Megan added.

"Yeah, me too," said Brett, more grudgingly.

Jim's face brightened, "Really? Then based on the Rule of 30, here is how much you should be setting aside for retirement." Jim looked around for another sheet of blank paper and then wrote out another table.

Table 7: Retirement saving as a balancing item (% of pay)

Ages (Brett)	Retirement saving
33–37	3%
38–42	19%
43–47	8%
48–52	8%
53–57	15%
58–62	30%

Brett and Megan tried to get closer to make out the numbers scrawled on the page.

"Just to make sure I understand," Brett started, "the percentages in Table 7 plus the last column of Table 6 always add up to 30 percent of pay?"

"Right," Jim confirmed.

"And the reason you do this," Megan continued, "is to ensure our spendable income doesn't get crowded out?"

"Right again. Except that the percentages shown in these tables are five-year averages because I didn't want to write it out year by year. In practice, you would recalculate the retirement saving percentage annually."

"Fine," replied Megan. "I see we would be saving just 3 percent of pay in the first five years!"

"Yes, assuming you have two children during that time. By the way, the five-year averages are masking some volatility. The Rule of 30 actually would have you saving only 1 percent of pay at ages 35 and 36."

Brett had other questions. "The low percentage in the first five years doesn't surprise me too much, but why does the saving rate skyrocket between ages 38 and 42?"

"It's because of the mortgage payments," explained Jim. "They dropped a little in dollar terms but a lot in percentage terms during the second five-year period because your pay was assumed to be much higher by then."

"Okay, and why does the saving rate then drop back down to just 8 percent between ages 43 and 47?"

"Again, it's all about the mortgage payments. Remember, I had you trading up to a more expensive house 10 years into the future. That raised your mortgage payments right back up to 25 percent, at least for one year."

While Brett digested this information, Megan raised the key question: "I can see the logic behind your idea of saving more when it's easier to save. But tell me, does this strategy — this Rule of 30 — ensure we save enough?"

Jim smiled. "You don't think I'd propose this if the answer were no, do you? But let's try it and see. We'll use the same scenario as before, meaning we'll assume that you'll be subject to the returns, interest rates and inflation from the period between 1946 and 1975. We'll add in early amortization of the mortgage. The other change is to replace the 12 percent retirement saving rate with a variable percentage using our new Rule of 30. Just like in Table 7."

Jim sat in front of the laptop for a few minutes to input some data into his spreadsheet. He then hit the "Enter" button and the printer started humming away. Seconds later, he handed out a new chart.

Jim explained, "This chart shows the new spending breakdown over your working careers. You can see that you won't be saving much before you're 40. As a result, we've improved your spendable income in your 30s.

Figure 7: Where the money goes (Rule of 30)

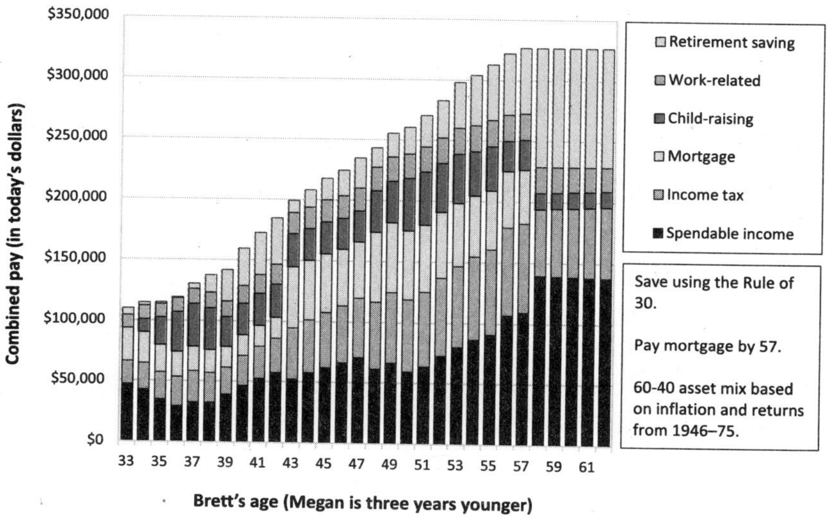

Legend:
- Retirement saving
- Work-related
- Child-raising
- Mortgage
- Income tax
- Spendable income

Save using the Rule of 30.

Pay mortgage by 57.

60-40 asset mix based on inflation and returns from 1946–75.

Y-axis: Combined pay (in today's dollars)

X-axis: Brett's age (Megan is three years younger) — 33, 35, 37, 39, 41, 43, 45, 47, 49, 51, 53, 55, 57, 59, 61

Even though you'll be saving much greater amounts from age 53 and on, you shouldn't feel the pinch. Your spendable income will be much higher in those years than it was in your 40s, even with the extra saving. I've also managed to keep the upward tilt in your spendable income as you get closer to retirement."

"That's good," said Brett, "but it doesn't prove that the saving strategy works. Don't we need to see how much retirement income we'd have under this Rule of 30?"

"Of course," said Jim, who was still sitting at the computer. A moment later, another chart came out of the printer. "This is what you're looking for." Jim handed Brett and Megan another chart.

Figure 8: Spendable income is less variable

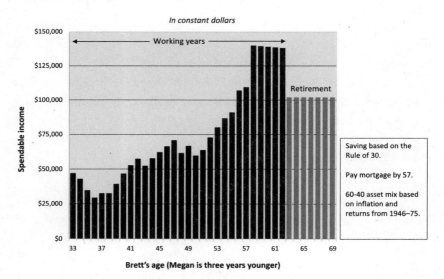

In constant dollars

Working years

Retirement

Saving based on the Rule of 30.

Pay mortgage by 57.

60-40 asset mix based on inflation and returns from 1946–75.

Spendable income

$150,000

$125,000

$100,000

$75,000

$50,000

$25,000

$0

33 37 41 45 49 53 57 61 65 69

Brett's age (Megan is three years younger)

"This is exactly the same as Figure 7 except that it's showing just spendable income, and I've also added spendable income in the first few years of retirement."

"Spendable income still drops a lot in retirement," Brett was quick to point out.

Megan chose to be more upbeat, "I agree it's not perfect, but it's better than it was."

"Don't get too fussed about the drop in spendable income after retirement," Jim advised. "We can and will address that. What is more important is that your spendable income is higher in retirement than it is in most of your working years.

"And that's not all. Notice how much more spendable income you now have in the critical early years. It's hard to see it from the charts I've shown you so far, so I've zeroed in on the years before age 50. This next chart shows your spendable income under both scenarios: if you save 12 percent a year versus if you save based on the Rule of 30."

Jim then presented them with yet another chart.

Brett studied Figure 9 intently. "I see that our spendable income isn't always higher if we save using the Rule of 30."

Figure 9: Rule of 30 produces smoother spendable income

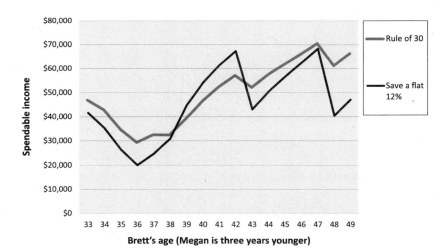

"That was never the goal," Jim replied. "The real point is that spendable income under the Rule of 30 is higher when you really need it to be higher. At age 36, for instance, it is now $30,000 instead of $20,000. And after the daycare years are over, spendable income rises fairly smoothly under the Rule of 30, more so than saving a flat 12 percent a year."

Brett wasn't easily derailed, "But even if we save based on the Rule of 30, Figure 8 is showing high spendable income between ages 58 and 62.

Isn't there a danger that we'll get used to spending at that level and go into shock once we retire?"

"It's a problem if we assume you follow the Rule of 30 to the letter right up until retirement age," replied Jim. "In fact, I see the Rule of 30 as something to guide you until you get into your mid-50s. After that, you should be using something like PERC to provide ongoing guidance as to how much you should be saving. PERC would show you that you ought to be contributing even more in the last five years. This action would reduce your spendable income to a level that you are more likely to be able to sustain after retirement. It also increases your retirement income."

"You've never mentioned PERC before," Megan noted. "What is it?"

"It stands for Personal Enhanced Retirement Calculator," Jim replied. "PERC will give you an estimate of how much retirement income you can generate from all sources. Once you start to close in on retirement, say when you're 10 years away, I would suggest that a calculator like PERC is a better way to determine your saving rate rather than strict adherence to the Rule of 30, or any other rule for that matter."

"Why is it better, Jim?" Megan asked.

"Because unlike any rule of thumb, PERC takes into account where you stand on your saving journey. It will let you know if you are on track or falling behind with your saving. It then lets you calculate how much you need to save to reach your ultimate goal.

"The Rule of 30, on the other hand, is designed to get you started on the right track and minimize the pain of saving. And as far as that goes, I think it does a very good job. Over a 30-year period, though, you have to expect some mid-course corrections. For instance, you might decide to bring your retirement date forward a year or two, or to push it back. Your assets might have soared during a recent bull market, or you might have suffered a big loss in a bear market. PERC allows you to fine-tune your saving rate to reflect all that."

Brett's eyes narrowed as he addressed Jim. "Are you trying to sell us something, Jim? What's the catch with this PERC?"

"No catch. It's free, and you won't get a sales call since you won't be providing any personal information. Frederick Vettese developed it with the IT team at Morneau Shepell, and they put it onto a Morneau Shepell–sponsored site as a service to the public. Big companies do that sometimes."

Brett and Megan both lapsed into silence, a sure sign that this session was drawing to a close.

Jim asked, "How are you feeling about the Rule of 30 now?"

Megan responded first. "It looks very promising, Jim, but I want to think about it."

Brett added, "No one has ever told us to make retirement spending a lesser priority before. Are you sure about all this?"

"The math behind the Rule of 30 is fairly straightforward," Jim replied. "And please, don't get the idea that I think saving for retirement is a low priority. Saving enough is still the primary goal of this exercise. Nevertheless, there will be times when saving won't be the very highest priority, especially when you're young. But I can see you still have reservations, and rightly so; I've presented a new idea and we need to make sure it works because the stakes are high. Therefore, I suggest we do some stress-testing."

"You don't think you've stressed us enough?" asked Megan with a smile.

"You know that's not what I mean," said Jim, smiling back. "We need to think of all the ways the Rule of 30 can go wrong and then troubleshoot. That'll be your homework for next week. I think we've done enough for one day."

Brett and Megan looked relieved, knowing they had survived another mind-bending session. They seemed to be making progress, but it was never easy. They went home with much to think about.

As Jim closed the door behind them, Megan whispered to Brett, "You know, Brett, I think Jim could use a whiteboard!"

A bit more about . . . PERC

PERC, or Personal Enhanced Retirement Calculator, is a tool that anyone can use, provided they are between ages 50 and 80. To use it, go online to perc.morneaushepell.com. It does not require you to enter any personal information that would allow someone to identify you (like name, employer, SIN, credit card number, etc.). You do have to enter information about your assets, your expected retirement age and your expected future contributions so that PERC can estimate how much retirement income you can expect.

The output from PERC includes three scenarios: (1) your retirement income based on a worst-case investment scenario and assuming no enhancements to your decumulation strategy; (2) retirement income based on the same worst-case scenario but assuming you adopt the first three enhancements described in the book *Retirement Income for Life (RIFL)*; and (3) retirement income based on a median investment scenario, including the three enhancements.

The worst-case and median investment scenarios represent the fifth-percentile and fiftieth-percentile returns based on a Monte Carlo simulation that was performed by Morneau Shepell. For the purposes of this book, it is the median scenario that forms the basis for determining how much spendable income you can expect in retirement.

Note that PERC does not directly calculate how much you should be saving in your remaining working years. You enter an amount to be saved (in RRSPs, TFSAs and non-tax-sheltered arrangements), and PERC shows the resulting retirement income. You would then do more than one iteration using trial and error until you achieve the desired retirement income.

You may be curious about the enhancements that underlie PERC. The first is to reduce fees. PERC assumes investment management fees (including advisor fees) reduce from 1.8 percent in the "before" scenario to 0.6 percent in the "after" scenario. The second enhancement is to defer CPP, usually until age 70, though it might be to some age between 65 and 70 if the amount of savings at retirement isn't enough to defer CPP all the way to 70. The third enhancement is to purchase an annuity (at the point of retirement) with 20 percent of one's tax-sheltered assets. This is essentially insurance against living longer than you expected.

Another unique aspect of PERC is the increases in income it assumes retirees will need. As is detailed in *RIFL*, the typical spending pattern for retirees is to increase their spending in line with inflation until their early 70s, after which spending will continue to increase in nominal terms but by less than the inflation rate. This tendency to spend less (in real terms) with age intensifies in one's 80s but then may start to rise again very late in life when retirement homes and personal support workers enter into the equation.

These enhancements and others are described in some detail in *Retirement Income for Life: Getting More without Saving More*, second edition.

CHAPTER 7

Stress-Testing the Rule of 30

Saturday, June 19

Brett and Megan arrived at Jim's door the following Saturday at 4 p.m. He greeted them cheerfully and then glanced down at Brett's side. "What do you have in that box?" he asked.

Jim was looking at a large flat package that Brett was carrying with outstretched arms. Brett brought it inside as Jim led them to the living room. With a flourish, Brett opened it up to reveal a new whiteboard, complete with dry erase markers still in their cellophane wrappers.

Jim's eyes lit up. "This is great! It will help us going forward, but what's the special occasion?"

Megan replied, "We wanted to wish you a happy Father's Day."

It was an awkward moment as Jim appeared to wince momentarily. After a brief hesitation, Jim politely thanked Megan and then moved on. As he propped the whiteboard on the fireplace mantel, he asked them, "Did you think of any ways in which the Rule of 30 might break down?"

Brett answered first. "That's all I could think about, actually. Let's start with my biggest worry. I'm uncomfortable with the fact that you're giving us carte blanche not to save."

"You think I'm giving you carte blanche?" asked Jim.

"I'm afraid I'll be able to find all sorts of 'extraordinary' expenses, as you call them, that will whittle our saving down to practically nothing. It is sort of like you've given us dispensation not to save."

"If that is your main worry, Brett, it means you have the right mind-set, so abusing the Rule of 30 is unlikely to be a problem for you. Saving always requires some discipline, which I think you have." Jim saw a look of doubt on Brett's face, so he added, "But I guess you're saying that having some leeway *not* to save makes it that much harder to stay on track. What should ease your mind is that we defined the sort of expense items that could offset saving rather stringently: the expense would have to be necessary, reasonably short in duration and easily quantifiable. Megan has already identified daycare as one potential item. Did you think of others that would qualify?"

"What about the children's education?" asked Megan. "Like university costs in 20 years' time or maybe private school, if we decide that's important?"

"I would argue that private schooling should not be deemed an absolute necessity, nor is it especially short-term in duration," replied Jim. "I would disqualify it as a saving offset on those grounds alone. It's fine if you can afford it, but not if it causes you to defer your retirement saving. As for university, it may be necessary, but you could always spread the cost of it over a longer period by contributing to an RESP, in which case it is just another component of child-raising costs and not an offset to saving. The cost of university doesn't have to be incurred over a short period. But I'm getting into the weeds now, and I don't want to obscure the good point you're making, Megan."

"Really? What good point was that?"

"That there will always be expenses that fall in a grey area — do you include them as offsets to retirement saving or don't you? Deciding can get tricky, and I'm not always going to be around to act as an adjudicator. We could make up a lot of rules, but I suspect that such an approach would become unwieldy in short order."

"What would we do, then?" asked Megan.

Jim collected his thoughts for a moment before responding. "I have a three-part response to this. First, the rules for including extraordinary expenses as offsets to retirement saving are already pretty clear. And while you might find a way around them and save less, there really is no incentive for you to 'game' the system. At the end of the day, you're only fooling yourself. If you have a good attitude toward saving, as you obviously do, then I don't think that applying the Rule of 30 sensibly is going to be a problem in practice.

"Second, applying the Rule of 30 eventually becomes a non-issue. As I mentioned last time, by the time retirement is maybe 10 years off, you'll have better ways to monitor whether you're on track with your saving. I mentioned PERC as an example. Once you start to use a calculator to figure out how much you should be saving in your final years, you wouldn't need to use the Rule of 30 anymore.

"Third, the Rule of 30 gives you a break in spending primarily in your early years, when the kids are in daycare. During these years, your income is likely to be a fair bit lower in real terms than what it will be later on in your lives. I've tested to see the effect of saving a few percentage points more in these early years, and the ultimate impact is minimal."

Jim paused for a moment and then asked, "Did you think of any other potential problems with the Rule of 30?"

Brett said, "Here is a really obvious one: couples without children. Their spendable income is going to be a lot higher, right? I have to believe they have to save more than the Rule of 30 would dictate."

Jim was ready for this one. "You know, Brett, that was initially my concern as well. But then it occurred to me that the years when child-raising costs are high tend to be the early years, when you're in your 30s or 40s. By the time you're into your 50s, the impact of child-raising costs is greatly reduced. This means that couples without children will have significantly higher spendable income than their child-bearing counterparts in the early years, but not so different as they approach retirement. This is key, since we ultimately want to have spendable income in retirement that matches our spendable income just before retirement. The other thing is that couples without children shouldn't see their saving rates reduced as much in the early years, because they have no daycare costs to offset the Rule of 30."

Brett looked disappointed. "It sounds like you talked the problem away, Jim."

Jim responded, "No, I was going to add that you are on to something. Couples without children definitely need to be saving more — just not as much more as you might think. If their investment returns aren't terrible, they can probably get away with adhering to the Rule of 30 and then saving a bit more if they have to when they get closer to retirement. But I wouldn't fault them for changing it to a Rule of 35."

Feeling a little pumped after this mini-victory, Brett decided to try again. "What if mortgage payments are really high? Not just 25 percent of pay, as in our case, but say more like 30 percent of pay? That would leave us with no room for retirement saving under the Rule of 30."

"If your mortgage payments are that high, and you plan to have children, it is telling me that you bought more home than you can afford," replied Jim. "Now, you might tell me you live in a city with such a crazy housing market that you had no choice but to pay that much. I can sympathize, but ultimately it means that saving adequately for retirement is going to become more of a challenge.

"Let me also point out that even if your mortgage payments start out at 30 percent, you'd still be able to save in subsequent years as your pay grows and mortgages become a smaller percentage of pay. This is especially true in periods of high inflation, as we saw in the first projection summarized in Table 2. Your mortgage payments started off at 25 percent of pay, but with some steep pay increases (remember we ran the projection through a high-inflation period), the same dollar payments dropped to just 11 percent of pay in the second five-year term of the mortgage.

"When inflation is lower and salaries are not rising as fast, the mortgage payments as a percentage of pay won't come down as quickly. Even this is less of a problem than it sounds because your retirement income target will be lower when inflation is lower; you could get away with a slightly lower saving rate. I know this isn't a perfect answer to your question, but you have to accept that if your mortgage payments are that high, it's bound to cause problems saving, no matter what rule you follow."

"What about the other extreme?" Brett asked. "What about savers who are lifetime renters, so they have no mortgage payments?"

"Good point, Brett, and I was eventually going to bring it up myself. I would apply the Rule of 30 to renters the same as owners, except that their rent would take the place of mortgage payments."

Megan this time, "But doesn't rent tend to be less than mortgage payments and wouldn't that mean that renters would be saving more than homeowners under the Rule of 30?"

"Is rent really less?" Jim questioned. "Take a condo in Toronto worth $500,000. You can expect monthly rent to be about $1,700 to $2,000. If you instead bought that condo with a $380,000 mortgage on it, your monthly mortgage payments would be about $1,700 based on the current low mortgage rates.

"And even if monthly rent is less than monthly mortgage payments in the future, that's okay, too. It would mean that renters would save more under the Rule of 30 than homeowners. That would be entirely appropriate, since renters would have more spendable income before retirement, which means higher spending expectations after retirement and the need to save more."

For a few moments, the room was silent. Jim asked again, "Anything else?"

Megan said, "I almost accepted a job with an employer who had a defined contribution pension plan. The employer was going to contribute 5 percent of pay into that plan on my behalf. How would that factor into the Rule of 30?"

"Easy," said Jim. "You would subtract the contribution the employer is making on your behalf when calculating your required retirement saving using the Rule of 30."

Brett changed the subject, "I'm still having a hard time accepting that we might not save for retirement at all in years when our other expenses are really high. Did you consider maybe revising the Rule of 30 to require a minimum saving rate, no matter what?"

"I did wonder about that, Brett. I tried changing my spreadsheet to require an RRSP contribution of at least 4 percent of pay, even in years when mortgage payments and daycare exceeded 30 percent. The main thing it did was reduce spendable income even further in the lean years when you couldn't afford to see it go lower, but it barely made a dent in the ultimate retirement income."

Being shot down again, Brett lapsed into silence.

"Surely people with higher income need to save a higher percentage," declared Megan. "After all, the CPP and OAS pensions make up a smaller fraction of the retirement income they'll need."

"You're partly right," Jim replied. "The fact that CPP and OAS provide a smaller proportion of their retirement income target does mean that they should be saving a higher percentage of pay, all things considered. On the other hand, high-net-worth households are probably paying a smaller percentage for investment management, so they get more mileage out of whatever they save.

"Another offsetting factor is that their mortgage payments are usually a smaller percentage of their income than is the case with lower-income households. Finally, most of them don't need to use up every penny of spendable income to live well. Even if their spendable income in retirement is a little lower than it was before retirement, it won't cause them any serious discomfort. The bottom line is that high-income households that save based on the Rule of 30 might ultimately wish they had contributed a couple of percentage points more, but they won't suffer either way."

Megan thought of another scenario, "What about retirement age? Surely you don't have to save as much if you retire at 70 instead of 60. Shouldn't this affect the Rule of 30?"

"You know, Megan, you could have been an actuary! You can indeed save less if you retire at 70 versus 60. I concede that for retirement at 70, maybe it should be the rule of 25, but I suggest sticking with the Rule of 30 even in that case."

"Why, Jim?" asked Megan. "You never struck me as overly cautious, especially for an actuary."

"There are several reasons," Jim replied. "First, it is simpler to have just one rule. Second, as I mentioned earlier, this Rule of 30 is most useful before you're 55 or so. We would use a different method to determine a saving rate when we get closer to retirement, so whether the magic number is 25 or 30 or 35 becomes a moot point at that stage. Third, you might plan to retire at age 70, but as John Lennon sang, life's what happens when you're busy making other plans. You might be forced to retire early, in which case you'd be happy you saved a little more."

Brett, who had been quiet for a while, rejoined the conversation. "I have to say, Jim, this all sounds a little too good to be true. You're telling us the Rule of 30 works if you start saving in your 30s or in your 40s, whether your income is really high or not so high, whether you're a renter or an owner, and so on."

"I'm not saying it's perfect," said Jim. "Far from it. I just think it's a lot better than trying to put aside a flat percentage of pay every year. When all is said and done, the purpose of the Rule of 30 is not to deliver the exact amount of income required at the point of retirement; its real purpose is to put you on the right track in the first two-thirds of your career while leaving you with a decent amount of spendable income. After that, more precise methods can bring you the rest of the way home."

Jim could sense the energy was seeping out of the room now. He knew it was time to wrap it up soon. "I think this has been a good session, but we're getting pretty close to the end. Can you think of any other possible problems with the Rule of 30?"

Brett again: "Surely the Rule of 30 can't work properly in the case of a couple who waits until past 40 to start saving seriously. I have a cousin, Jeff, who's 42, and I know he and his wife haven't saved much at all."

"If he were in his late 40s when he started to save," Jim replied, "I would totally agree with you. Every rule of thumb has its limits, and people should know there are consequences to starting too late to save. By his late 40s, he would probably have reached the point where he has to reduce spending and save every spare dime.

"But since your cousin is in his early 40s," Jim continued, "the Rule of 30 should work for him, too.[1] This is based on the assumptions that (a) Jeff and his wife are past the daycare stage and (b) are less likely than you to trade up to a bigger home between now and retirement. As a result, they should have a relatively high capacity to save from here on in. I'm also assuming that they are prepared to stay in the workforce at least a couple of years longer to make up for lost time. What else?"

Brett was starting to feel this was like a tennis match, with Jim hitting the ball back to his side of the court no matter what Brett threw his way.

---

[1]   For the readers who are like Jeff, please see the sidebar at the end of this chapter.

He decided to change his approach. "Can I ask, then, what you see as the biggest test for the Rule of 30?"

"We've already discussed the relevance of the Rule of 30 if you retire much later, like at age 70," began Jim. "What I see as a bigger problem is if you are forced to retire much earlier than planned. As with everything else in life, one's retirement plans do not always pan out. Unplanned early retirement represents one of the biggest challenges to saving for retirement. This is true no matter what rule you follow to save, but it may be a bigger problem with the Rule of 30, since that rule tends to backload your retirement saving."

"Backload?"

"You know, skew most of your heavy saving toward your last few years of work," said Jim, who noticed Megan was looking a little more tired than usual today. "I want to make sure this issue gets enough air time so why don't we leave that until next time? Same time next Saturday?"

As much as Megan enjoyed these sessions, she was a little relieved that this particular one was over. "Thank you again for all this. We learn something every time we see you. But you never let us go home without something to worry about, do you?"

Jim laughed at this. "I would prefer to categorize it as 'something to think about.' In any event, we are making good progress. Thanks again for the whiteboard! Until next time, then?"

A bit more about . . . Applying the Rule of 30 to 40-somethings

Does the Rule of 30 apply to someone who starts saving in their early 40s? To examine this question, we will consider the situation of Brett's cousin, Jeff.

Jeff is 42 and is earning $100,000. His wife, Sandra, is 39 and earns $75,000 a year. They have two children who have consumed most of their energy and disposable income over the last 10 years. They saved a little but also splurged on a few vacations and "toys," like a secondhand BMW Z4. Whatever spare money they had went into mortgage payments on their first house, which they bought nine years ago. They just bought their second house for $1 million, against which they applied the equity they had built up in their first home, an amount of $360,000. Their mortgage payments started at 28 percent of their combined income but slowly dropped in percentage terms in subsequent years as their employment income grew. The house will be fully paid off by the time Jeff reaches 60.

So far, Jeff and Sandra have managed to save a mere $30,000 for retirement, which they know puts them well behind schedule. They should be able to save more in future years, since their daycare years are long behind them and they have no plans to buy a more expensive home. The other positive is that they have reconciled themselves to working until 65 rather than 63 like cousin Brett; this is the price they pay for waiting so long to save.

For the next 23 years, Jeff and Sandra save for retirement based on the Rule of 30. Once again, we pick a very poor historic period for investment purposes — the one ending in 1975 — to test their retirement readiness. In spite of the shortened saving period and the poor investment returns, their financial position going into retirement at age 65 is not dire. As Figure 10 shows, their spendable income after retirement is comparable to what it was in their last year of work, and more (even in real terms) than at almost any other point in their lives. However, they did have to increase their saving rate by another 3 percent in their last five years of work to accomplish this result.

This example demonstrates that the Rule of 30 can be useful for the cohort that really needs to know how much to save: those aged 30 to 45. Before 30, any saving that is done is a bonus. Barring a sizable inheritance, anyone who starts to save later than 45 will probably have to put aside every last dime rather than relying on any saving rule.

One reason that the Rule of 30 can apply over such a broad range of ages is that not much saving is expected from people in their 30s because of other expenses. In addition, no saving rule is precise, given the possible range in investment results, salary increases, inflation rates and retirement ages. The Rule of 30 is essentially a way to save until age 55, at which point a more precise calculation can be made of the required saving rate with the use of a retirement calculator.

Figure 10: Jeff and Sandra start late but can still retire well

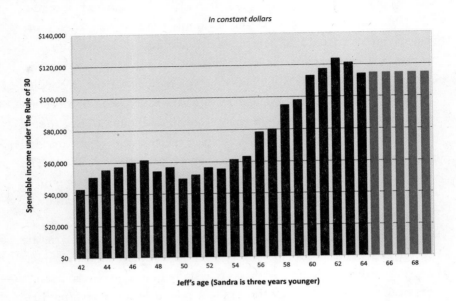

In constant dollars

Spendable income under the Rule of 30 / Jeff's age (Sandra is three years younger)

CHAPTER 8

The Vulnerable Years

Saturday, June 26

The next Saturday, they had to meet in the morning instead of the afternoon because of a scheduling conflict. Brett and Megan showed up at Jim's doorstep at 9 a.m.

As Jim ushered them in, he noticed Megan looked a little pale. "Everything okay with you, Megan?" Jim asked.

"Oh, not to worry," she shrugged with a smile. "Maybe it was something I ate, but it's no big deal."

"I hope this retirement planning isn't taking its toll," Jim replied, with some concern in his voice. "Anyway, my plan today is to close the loop on the Rule of 30. We showed it would work pretty well for you, and it should work well in most special situations, too. What I didn't mention last time is that there is an added bonus in using the Rule of 30 to determine your RRSP contributions."

Brett perked up. "Really? What's that?"

"You end up making heavier contributions in the years when you have more spendable income. Those also happen to be years when your gross income is higher. That means you'll have a higher marginal tax rate in those years."

Brett cocked his head to one side. "Okay, I'm barely following. How is that good?"

"Take your situation," Jim replied. "I estimate that your combined marginal tax rate currently is 25 percent, but with promotions and such, it will rise to about 40 percent by the time you retire. If you contribute $10,000 now to an RRSP, you get back $2,500 as a tax refund. If you contribute the same $10,000 later when your marginal tax rate is 40 percent, you'll get a refund of $4,000."

Brett's eyes lit up, "Right! So, the net cost is only $6,000 instead of $7,500!"

"That's right," Jim confirmed. "Now I'm going to switch gears on you and bring up the biggest challenge to the Rule of 30."

"Uh, oh," said Megan, "this sounds ominous."

"It's nothing we can't handle," Jim assured her. "The Rule of 30 will usually create an uneven pattern of saving, but this is intentional, since the goal is to minimize the ups and downs in your spendable income, not the ups and downs in your saving. As I mentioned last time, your retirement saving rate will tend to rise under the Rule of 30 as you get closer to retirement. This is partly because mortgage payments tend to shrink as a percentage of pay as you get older. Also, you don't have to worry about daycare expenses after a certain age.

"Backloading your retirement saving is fine as long as you can keep working full-time until your planned retirement age. The problem is that your work plans might change."

"Oh, I'm quite committed to working into my 60s," said Brett.

"You might be," Jim replied, "but that doesn't mean you will. The Society of Actuaries conducted a study of retirees and pre-retirees a few years ago and found that the pre-retirees planned to retire at age 65, on average. As for the people in the survey who were already retired, the average age at which they retired was 58. Think about that. People think they're going to retire at 65, but people actually retired at 58. That's a gap of seven years."

"Could it be that the people who are currently in the workforce just plan to work longer than used to be the case?" Megan ventured.

"That could be a factor," Jim conceded, "and it may even account for one or two years of that seven-year discrepancy. But it almost certainly doesn't account for most of it."

"What does, then?" Megan asked.

Jim explained. "There are two big reasons why people retire earlier than planned. The first is that their employer pushes them out. It is common practice for companies to incentivize older employees to leave. Sometimes this happens through voluntary early retirement packages that are offered to a broad group of older employees, and sometimes the employer will target specific people or maybe just one person. Either way, the end result is that many employees find themselves ushered out the door years before they planned to leave on their own."

"Why would companies force their older employees to leave?" asked Megan. "They are the ones with all the experience and maturity. That should count for something, no?"

"Older employees are still valuable for the reasons you mention," said Jim, nodding, "but employers sometimes see the negatives as outweighing the positives. It's a fact that workers become more expensive with age. For years or even decades, they would have been receiving pay increases in excess of price inflation. This eventually adds up to a big number. They also become entitled to four weeks of vacation or more, versus the two or maybe three weeks given to a new employee. Their health benefits are also a lot more expensive.

"But it's not just that. Productivity and effectiveness start to tail off eventually. Workers in their 50s are often less willing or able to maintain the long hours of work and intensity they had exhibited in their earlier days. Their skill set may become a little dated, too, as they find it harder to learn new ways of doing things, especially if it involves technology. Besides that, they're simply more resistant to change, something employers can find frustrating when they are trying to implement new policies or procedures. I don't necessarily agree with this characterization, but this type of thinking exists, nonetheless. Employers just don't talk about it publicly.

"By the way," Jim continued, "I had firsthand experience of what it's like to be on the receiving end. The consulting firm where I had worked for 20 years gave me a significant financial incentive to leave about five years ago, a little sooner than I had planned to retire. Could I have fought it? Probably not, since it might have involved going to court to prove the severance wasn't enough, and would I really want to stay with the company after that? Besides, maybe we wouldn't have been able to do these sessions!"

"Well, that's one good thing, at least," offered Megan.

Brett, as usual, was still turning Jim's earlier arguments over in his mind. He said, "No matter what, a worker who is nearing 60 is still worth something. Maybe they're 10 percent less productive than they used to be, maybe 20 percent, I don't know. Can't the company just reduce their compensation by that percentage, so they still feel they're getting value for their money?"

"That's harder to do than you might think," said Jim. "First and foremost, if the employer approaches a given employee and asks him to take a pay cut, it is deemed to be constructive dismissal. The employer can get into all kinds of legal trouble by doing that. Second, even if the employee made the first move, the two parties are unlikely to agree on what constitutes a fair pay cut. Finally, it may cause a morale problem for younger full-time employees. They see old Jim not working as hard as he used to and taking a couple of afternoons off every week to play golf, but they may not be aware of the pay cut he took as a result.

"In a nutshell, early retirement has been a very common practice for decades. It's unlikely to disappear anytime soon, or maybe ever. Unfortunately, once you lose your regular full-time job, you are very unlikely to find another one, or at least one that pays nearly as well. In most cases, the best you can hope for is to work freelance or on a contract basis, and even then, you will probably make less money. Usually much less."

Jim paused while Brett and Megan absorbed this sobering news. Then he continued, "But even if you're one of the lucky ones whose employer wants you to stick around, you might still find yourself out of work for another reason."

"That other reason being?" asked Megan.

"Your health," said Jim. "In general, we are living longer, but not necessarily healthier. People who may have been healthy their entire lives are still vulnerable to a host of critical illnesses once they turn 50. By 60, it's even worse. It has been estimated that a healthy 50-year-old male has nearly a chance in two of contracting a critical illness or dying before he turns 70."[1]

"Not good! What constitutes a critical illness?" asked Megan.

"This would be something serious like heart disease, cancer, Parkinson's or Alzheimer's. Some rather serious problems like severe arthritis, diabetes or chronic back pain don't even qualify as critical illnesses, which gives you an idea of what you're up against."

"A chance in two, eh?" Brett repeated incredulously.

"Yes," said Jim, "life can throw you some pretty nasty curves. Your retirement planning needs to take them into account."

"What are you saying, then," asked Brett, "that we shouldn't count on those last five or so years of work when we are doing our retirement planning?"

"I wouldn't go that far," said Jim. "In the first case, where your employer simply doesn't want you anymore, you might be entitled to significant severance pay and that'll soften the financial blow. Also, you are likely to find some temporary employment if you really want it. In the case of poor health, you should have disability income insurance — either individually or through your workplace — which will help tide you over. You would be a little reckless to act as if no problems will ever befall you, but I wouldn't overdo the pessimism."

"What do you suggest, then?" asked Brett.

"I would do a little discounting of future earnings, but this can vary from one person to the next. In your case, there are two of you, so it is likely that one of you will escape unscathed. I might assume that your combined pay in your last five years will be 30 percent less than you would otherwise project. Shall we test this?"

Jim then started to map out the projection he had in mind. "Let's start by assuming nothing changes up until age 58 for Brett and 55 for Megan. Until then, you're saving based on the Rule of 30 and you have just finished paying off your mortgage. Then, in the years from 58 to 62, one of you (we won't say who) loses the full-time job you had held for many years.

---

[1]   The odds are a little better for women. Readers might turn to the chapters on critical illness in my book *The Essential Retirement Guide*.

Since that person might still find some work, let's assume your combined income is 70 percent as much as you had previously earned.

"At the point your pay was reduced, you might have been spending a modest amount on the children for incidentals like cell phone bills or help with the rent. Even though your own financial situation has deteriorated, you might still feel inclined to help them out but to a lesser extent, since you now have financial issues of your own."

Brett jumped in, "I guess the kids will have to learn to fend for themselves just a little sooner. I don't see that as a bad thing."

"I'd go a step further," said Jim. "I would say that taking steps in your children's early years to foster their independence later on could be the most important retirement planning advice I can give you!"

"I'll remember that," murmured Megan.

Brett was already looking at the printer, "When you make all those changes, where does that leave us?"

Jim picked up a piece of paper from the table. "I've produced a new chart that is similar to Figure 8 but with the changes I just described. I did all that before you came today, so here is the result." With that, Jim produced Figure 11.

Brett and Megan just stared at it for about 30 seconds before Megan spoke up. "This doesn't look bad at all."

Jim remarked, "You'll notice something special about your spendable income in the last five years before retirement."

Brett and Megan stared at the chart for a while longer. Finally, Megan said, "Oh, I see what you mean! In those last five years, our earnings dropped a lot, but our *spendable* income is about the same as it was before the drop. What magic did you use to make that happen?"

"First of all, that's around the time the mortgage payments disappear. In addition, all the other spending items that offset spendable income have dropped as a direct result of having reduced income: child costs, retirement saving and income tax. This is why you can maintain your spendable income. Since you're not saving quite as much for retirement, though, you have to expect the end result to be a little worse than if your income had never dropped. Here's the good news: your spendable income in retirement is higher than it was at any other time in your life up until age 55."

"I guess that's a pretty good result, given the circumstances," said Brett.

Figure 11: Spendable income with lower pay in last five years

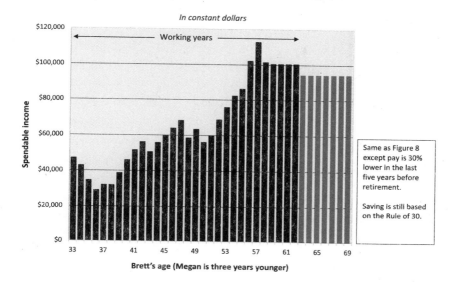

In constant dollars

Working years →

Spendable income

$120,000
$100,000
$80,000
$60,000
$40,000
$20,000
$0

33 37 41 45 49 53 57 61 65 69

Brett's age (Megan is three years younger)

Same as Figure 8 except pay is 30% lower in the last five years before retirement.

Saving is still based on the Rule of 30.

"Even then, we can still do a little better," Jim offered.

"You have some magic tricks up your sleeve to boost our retirement income?" asked Megan.

"It's not so magical. I'm talking about changing your asset mix. We'll get to that very soon, just not today."

Brett, in the meantime, was back studying Figure 11. He asked, "Jim, is this why you recommended we pay off the mortgage early?"

"Absolutely. In those last five years when your combined earnings were 30 percent lower, making big mortgage payments would have been a challenge, to say the least. You might have been forced to downsize. Of course, having the peace of mind of a paid-off home came at a price; your spendable income was a little less throughout your working years than it would have been, except of course for the last five years of work when you had no mortgage."

As usual, Brett wasn't quite persuaded. "Wouldn't we be in the same place, though, if we had paid off the mortgage more slowly and saved more for retirement throughout?"

"In some ways, yes, since saving for retirement and paying the mortgage on your home are very similar actions: both involve setting aside money now for a more secure future. But it would have been more difficult for the two of you to cope if the mortgage wasn't fully paid by the time your income dropped, so I still see paying it off early as the better option."

At this point, Jim suddenly seemed lost deep in thought, as if he were debating whether or not to say something else. He finally decided. "I have to admit, this example is a little too neat. I arranged it so the mortgage was paid off precisely when your income dropped. In real life, things tend to be messier. For instance, you might not have quite finished making payments when your employer pulled the rug out from under your feet. Nevertheless, that doesn't change the basic approach."

"What about if our income in those last five working years doesn't fall after all?" asked Megan. "Doesn't paying off the mortgage early mean we lowered our spendable income during all those early years for nothing?"

"Not for nothing. Paying the mortgage early is like insurance against possible loss of income, except that the 'insurance premiums' stay in your pocket. As I just mentioned, mortgage payments and retirement saving are nearly equivalent. If you pay the mortgage off early, you can save more for retirement later on. You still end up in practically the same place. This route just happens to be more conservative, since you make your mortgage payments with after-tax dollars."

Brett and Megan lapsed into silence. Brett stretched. They could sense that the daily session was coming to an end.

Megan asked Jim, "What's the major takeaway today?"

"Even if your career ends a little sooner than you planned, you can still save enough for a comfortable retirement," he replied. "Having said that, there is no escaping the fact that you need employment income to create retirement income. If your employment income is reduced for some reason, it can't help but affect your retirement as well. All I'm doing here is trying to mitigate the problem, but it doesn't go away entirely."

"What's next on the agenda?" asked Megan.

"I mentioned the importance of asset mix. It's a way to boost your retirement income a little without having to save more."

Megan wanted to know, "Are we saying goodbye, then, to the 60-40 asset mix that you've been using?"

"As a matter of fact, we are," confirmed Jim. "Shall we take this up again next Saturday at four o'clock, as usual?"

Brett and Megan agreed and returned home. As they left, Jim meticulously wiped his new whiteboard clean and put it away.

CHAPTER 9

Using Asset Mix to Improve Returns

Saturday, July 9

It was actually two weeks before they could meet again, since Brett and Megan went out of town to visit Megan's mother in Orangeville for the long Canada Day weekend. (Megan's dad had died three years earlier.) When they did meet the following Saturday, Megan had brought something in a box.

"What do we have here?" Jim asked.

Megan opened the box to reveal a cake. Jim laughed when he saw that the top of it was decorated like a pie chart, with 60 percent covered in chocolate icing and the other 40 percent in vanilla.

Megan explained, "The whiteboard was more for us than for you, so I wanted to make up for it. I was going to make a cake anyway, and at the last minute I got the idea of turning it into an asset-mix cake. From what you were telling us, it sounded like we wouldn't be seeing the 60-40 asset mix much longer, so I decided to give it a proper send-off. What will it be, chocolate side or vanilla?"

As Megan started to cut pieces for everyone, Jim began his weekly talk.

"You are quite correct in noting that all the asset projections I've done so far have been based on a 60-40 asset mix. In pension circles, 60-40 has been the default asset mix, at least here in Canada. That's what pension fund managers have been using year in and year out for most defined benefit pension plans since at least the 1960s."

"And that's why you've been assuming a 60-40 asset mix in all the work you've done so far?" Brett asked.

"Yes," replied Jim, "but it was never meant to be any more than a placeholder. Today, we're going to investigate whether it makes sense to be more heavily weighted in stocks."

Megan shifted a little in her chair. "I should have said this before, Jim, but I've never been comfortable with the idea of investing in the stock market. Stocks seem like such a gamble. I think of Bre-X or Nortel, for example. Or GameStop. I knew we couldn't avoid stocks entirely in our portfolio, but now you're suggesting we should invest even more than 60 percent. Shouldn't we be more careful with our retirement money?"

Jim did his actuarial best to show empathy. "I know how you must feel, Megan. A lot of people are uncomfortable with stocks and, yes, they can be risky. If you have a long-term investment horizon, however, much of that risk is an illusion."

"How do you mean?" asked Megan.

"Stocks look risky to many people because they can produce losses over the short term, by which I mean a period of up to several years. From this perspective, stocks *will* seem quite risky, even if you buy into an equity fund that simply tracks a benchmark index like the S&P/TSX in Canada or the S&P 500 in the United States.

"In every decade, there has been at least one year, and more often three, in which that equity fund would have delivered a negative return. This has been true for the past century at least, and probably longer. In two of those decades, the 1930s and the 1960s, the major stock markets produced negative returns in *four* out of the 10 years — and that's after including the dividends that stocks pay out! Sometimes, the negative returns reached double digits."

"Lovely," murmured Megan.

"On the other hand," Jim went on, "stocks have delivered amazingly good returns over the long term. If you think in terms of decades instead of years, the risks in the market start to fade away. The longer you hold stocks, the more likely they are to provide a steady return. As Jeremy Siegel shows in his book *Stocks for the Long Run*, one dollar invested in the US stock market back in 1802 would have grown by 2001 to $8.8 million!"

Megan whistled. "Just one dollar invested at the beginning of that period?"

"That's right, Megan. Now, that growth includes two centuries' worth of inflation, but even if we back that out, one dollar still grew in real terms to $599,605 over that period. That's the magic of compounding for you!"

"And in Canada?"

"We don't have Canadian data going back as far as that, but it does go back to 1924. One dollar invested in Canadian stocks at the start of 1924 grew by the end of 2019 to $6,610. This is if you had invested in the main stock index, so I'm not assuming you got lucky and picked a highflier."

"What is the main index in Canada, anyway?" asked Megan.

"It used to be called the Toronto Stock Exchange, or TSE, and it was created in 1861. The TSE 300 Composite Index (which tracks the three hundred companies on the exchange with the highest market capitalization) was launched in 1977. The TSE was then rebranded as the TSX in 2002. Its main index is maintained on an ongoing basis by Standard & Poor's, which is why it is known as the S&P/TSX."

"Anyway," said Jim, getting back on track, "that $6,610 pot of gold at the end of the rainbow includes nearly a century of inflation, but if we strip out inflation, that one dollar still grew in real terms to $445."

Megan shook her head in disbelief, "But surely you must have left out the great stock market crash."

"You mean the one that began in 1929?" Jim asked. "You would think so, given that Canadian stocks dropped 65 percent over the four calendar years from 1929 to 1932, and US stocks dropped even more. But no, the full effect of the crash is included in the numbers. So, of course, are all the other bear markets that have occurred since the 1920s."

Brett had been deep in thought for the last few minutes; he finally spoke up. "I'm having a hard time getting my mind around such big accumulations, Jim. Can you translate those numbers into annual returns?"

"Certainly. The average real return for US stocks over the two hundred–year period ending in 2001 was 6.7 percent a year. For Canadian stocks, the average real return from 1924 to 2019 has been 6.6 percent. As an aside, it's almost uncanny to me that a different stock market in a different country over a different period produces almost the same real return. It's almost like there is a law governing successful capitalism."

"Those are great returns," Brett conceded, "but I see one problem with your analysis. We're not going to live another hundred years!"

"Your investment horizon certainly isn't that long, I agree, but it is at least 30 years. That is how long you have to invest until you retire. (We'll ignore the investment period after retirement, since that is a separate issue.) You'll be happy to learn that the lowest real return on Canadian stocks over any 30-year period since 1924 was 3.6 percent a year. That happened from 1965 to 1994. It doesn't mean that the return you'll achieve in the future can't go lower, but it's nice to know that it never has."

"Maybe Canada and the US are special cases?" Megan wondered aloud.

"That's an interesting question," said Jim thoughtfully. "I would say Canada and the US are both unusually fortunate in that they have not experienced a war on their soil in over two hundred years. Stock prices in Germany plummeted by at least 90 percent around the end of World War II, but they did ultimately recover. If you go all the way back to 1925 and measure returns up to 2001, the average compounded real return on German equities was still 6.44 percent, virtually the same as in Canada and the US. German stocks have continued to do well since then; in the 18 years since the beginning of 2002, the German DAX (its main index) has quadrupled. You also have to add in dividends earned during that time to work out the total return."

"What about the UK?"

"Pretty much the same story," said Jim. "In the same 75-year period ending in 2001, the average real return on UK stocks was 6.01 percent. This isn't bad considering that the British Empire was in decline for pretty much the entire period. I admit, the FTSE (the main UK index) hasn't done as well as the DAX since 2001. Maybe that's because of Brexit, but it's still up considerably."

"What you're saying is that stocks have done well pretty much everywhere."

"At least in developed countries," Jim confirmed, "with the possible exception of Japan, but we'll get into that later."

"What about bonds?" asked Megan.

"There are many different types of bonds," Jim replied. "Foreign, domestic, corporate, short-term and long-term. Let's focus on long-term Government of Canada bonds, since they are essentially risk-free and may be most suitable to a long-term investment horizon. I'll refer to them as 'long-Canada' bonds.

"Long-Canada bonds are expected to produce a significantly lower return than stocks over the long run. That is because they are less risky, or at least that is the perception. Over shorter periods, bond prices are less volatile than stocks, so they do seem less risky. But the longer your investment horizon, the less appealing bonds will look compared to stocks. Over the longest period we can measure, from 1924 to 2019, the average compounded return on bonds in real terms has been 3.1 percent."[1]

Brett reacted to this last comment, "Then why would anyone invest in bonds?"

"Bonds act as a rudder for the portfolio," Jim explained. "They offer some stability during those times when the stock market plummets, like it did in 1973–74. This is especially relevant for the particular period I chose, since your portfolio would have shrunk nearly 21 percent over those two years when you were just one year away from retirement."

"Even with a 60-40 mix?" exclaimed Brett. "The rudder must have been broken."

Jim shrugged. "The loss would have been 33 percent if you had been invested 100 percent in stocks in those two years."[2]

Brett didn't back down. "Fair enough, but it still sounds like bonds act more as a brake than a rudder most of the time."

"Well, that's why we're having this talk today and why I'm going to propose a change in asset mix."

"I still don't get it," Brett went on. "If these professional fund managers have a long-term investment horizon, shouldn't they invest more in stocks, too?"

---

1   Based on buying long-Canada bonds on December 31 of the preceding year and selling on the same date in the current year. The return includes both coupons plus the gain or loss on the price change.

2   Jim is assuming half the stocks would track the S&P/TSX and the other half the S&P 500.

"They probably should, if they really did have a very long-term horizon," replied Jim. "But the fact is, managers need to show results over periods much shorter than that if they want to keep their clients happy. The performance of managers is usually assessed on a rolling four-year period, and if their returns aren't good enough, the manager might be replaced. If the bonds reduce overall returns a little in good times, they make up for it by propping up returns, at least a little, in the years when stock market returns are negative.

"But you make a good point, Brett. You should care a lot less about how your portfolio performs over short periods and a lot more about where you're going to be at retirement. As we'll see later, it's a near-certainty that bonds will not produce anywhere close to a 3 percent real return over the next 30 years. Even when bonds did relatively well, stocks were a better place to be. To prove it, let's take a look back in history and see just how smart it was to maintain a 60-40 asset mix. We will compare it to a portfolio that is 100 percent stocks."

Jim handed out a chart labelled Figure 12. "You will have seen the green line on this chart before. It came from Figure 1, the chart that showed both the real and the nominal return on a 60-40 asset mix over 30-year periods. This time, we're showing just real returns, so we don't turn the chart into

Figure 12: 100 percent stocks is usually better than 60-40

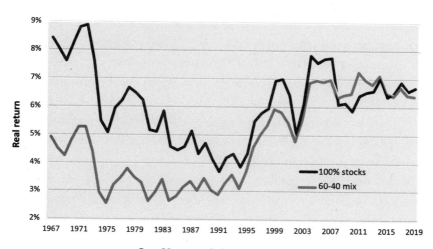

Over 30-year periods ending in year shown

spaghetti with too many lines. When you look at Figure 12, what else do you see?"

Brett answered, "As you say, stocks have been the place to be, at least most of the time."

"That's right," Jim confirmed. "The only two 30-year periods when a 60-40 mix was better were 1982 to 2011 and 1983 to 2012, and given the 29-year overlap between them, it's really more like one period. Can you think of why the 60-40 mix would have performed better over the periods ending in 2011 or 2012?"

Megan answered this one. "It was right after the global financial meltdown that occurred in 2008–09. I guess stocks hadn't fully recovered yet from that bear market."

"That's right," verified Jim, "though it's only part of the answer. The other part is that bonds did something extraordinary during that period. The yields on long-term Canada bonds fell from 14.3 percent in 1982 to 3.2 percent in 2011. That's a drop of more than 11 percentage points! Since bonds produce capital gains only when yields fall, the huge drop in yields resulted in unprecedented capital gains over that period. That literally can't happen again over the next 30 years, since bond yields are so low right now."

"Are you saying it's better to invest 100 percent of our savings in stocks?" asked Megan, a little skeptical.

"As a matter of fact, yes, as long as you have a 30-year investment horizon. That is what you have today; longer, actually, if we include some of the years after you retire. But your investment horizon won't always be that long, so to be safe, you need to keep on adjusting your asset mix by moving money into bonds little by little in future years."

"It sounds like we will really need to be on top of our portfolio," said Brett.

"There is a way to make the transition to bonds more automatic," said Jim. "Many investment firms and insurance companies offer something known as target date funds, or TDFs for short. These funds start with a heavy weighting in equities and then slowly increase the weighting in bonds over a period of many years. For instance, a target date fund based on retirement in 2055 might have an 85-15 asset mix today; the exact mix varies from one company to the next. As you get closer to 2055, that mix will slowly change to something like 50-50.

"The advantage of investing in TDFs is that you don't have to worry about changing your asset mix over time. The fund managers will do it for you automatically. The main disadvantage is that TDFs tend to be more expensive than if you try to manage the asset mix yourself using low-cost ETFs. The other disadvantage is that you might think the asset mix in a particular TDF is too conservative."

"Could you map out for us what type of asset mix we would invest in between now and retirement if we take this TDF approach?" asked Megan.

"Sure. Let's write it out on my whiteboard."

As Megan nodded approvingly, Jim wrote the following:

Table 8: A TDF approach to asset mix

Years to retirement	Asset mix (stocks-bonds)
30	100-0
25	90-10
20	80-20
15	70-30
10	60-40
0	50-50

Megan stared pensively at the board. "You won't be surprised to hear me say this, but your recommended equity weightings seem a little aggressive. Are you sure it's a good idea to invest this much in stocks?"

Jim said, "I would point out that you cannot use the word 'sure' when you talk about anything related to future investment performance. My recommendation is indeed a little more heavily weighted toward equities than the average target date fund, but I think that's appropriate. It is based on the fact that interest rates are so low right now that the prospects of a decent return on bonds are very slim. Nevertheless, this recommendation is the type of thing you play by ear. If bond yields make a strong upward move in the coming years, then it could make sense to increase your weighting in bonds, but only after that upward move has happened." Jim added with a shrug, "Even then, I'm not sure I'd steer too much off this particular path."

Brett and Megan didn't know what to say. There was a brief lull in the conversation as they mulled over Jim's words in their heads.

Jim broke the silence. "Perhaps I can show you something that will make you feel better about using a gradually shifting asset mix. Let's see what happens if we apply the TDF approach to the worst 30-year investment period in history, the period from 1946 to 1975."

"Our old standby!" Megan exclaimed.

"Yes, the very one. Our starting point is Figure 11 from the other day. It showed your spendable income before and after retirement in the scenario where your earnings fell 30 percent for your last five working years. That chart was based on a 60-40 asset mix and it showed that your spendable income fell a little after retirement. Does that ring a bell?"

Brett and Megan both nodded.

"Now, let's do that projection again, but this time assuming your asset mix changes over time as shown in Table 8." Jim worked his magic on his laptop. Within minutes, he had results. "By changing to a TDF approach to asset mix, your assets would be 17 percent higher after 30 years versus using a 60-40 asset mix."

"Impressive," Brett replied, but he wasn't quite convinced yet. "Perhaps the 1946–75 period was unusually good for a TDF approach to investing. Did you try any other period, especially one that doesn't overlap with those years?"

"As a matter of fact," said Jim, "I also made a calculation for the period 1976 to 2005. It was a very different period, since it started with high inflation and high interest rates, both of which eventually dropped substantially by the end of the period."

"What were the results?"

"The accumulation using the TDF approach was 21 percent higher."

Brett reacted as if he had just remembered something important. "Wait a minute, Jim. Weren't you showing us that over the 30-year period ending in 2011, bonds beat stocks? Wouldn't a 60-40 mix have been better than the TDF approach for that period at least? Why didn't you use that?"

"As a matter of fact," Jim explained, "I did try 1982 to 2011, too. And yes, the gap between the TDF approach and a straight 60-40 mix was indeed smaller than for the other periods. But even then, the TDF approach was a little better. As for why I didn't use that period instead of 1976 to 2005, it's because it wasn't representative of anything you can expect going forward. It was literally a once-in-a-century phenomenon given the 11-point drop in bond yields.

"The fact is, yields now have nowhere to go but up (or maybe sideways), which means bonds can't reproduce the returns they had then. If a 60-40 mix didn't beat the TDF approach during 1982 to 2011, it's a safe bet it won't do so during your lifetime."

"Are you sure?" asked Brett.

"There's that word again!" said Jim. "I swear, we're going to have to start doing tequila shots every time someone asks me if I'm sure."

Megan laughed. "You're assuming the stock markets don't tank?"

"Yes, I'm *reasonably confident* that stocks are not going to deliver a negative real return over a 30-year period given that they never have done so in the past. We will eventually discuss just what we can expect in terms of future stock and bond returns. When we do, we'll find that the TDF approach is still the way to go."

Brett, however, was not done yet. "Sorry for belabouring the issue, but if stocks are so much better than bonds, then why don't you stick with 100 percent in stocks for the entire 30-year period?"

Jim responded patiently, "It's because your investment horizon is continually shrinking over that time. By the time you're 53, for instance, you'll have only 10 years to go to retirement. There have been many 10-year periods where stocks have done much worse than bonds, and so adding bonds to the portfolio helps to limit the potential damage at a time in life when you have a diminished tolerance for risk. What I'm trying to do is get you safely to your retirement date with enough money for the two of you to be comfortable for the rest of your lives."

Brett finally appeared to be satisfied. Today's session was a little longer than usual, but it didn't feel that way to Brett and Megan. This was maybe the first time that Jim delivered only good news. As they were exiting the living room, Megan quietly put a smiley face on Jim's whiteboard.

CHAPTER 10

Refinements to Your Investing Approach

Saturday, July 16

They were now in the dog days of summer. It was unusually hot when Brett and Megan walked over to Jim's house the following Saturday afternoon.

On the way there, Megan looked pensive. "Brett, why do you think Jim is prepared to spend so much time helping us with our retirement planning? I mean, I'm glad about it, but he barely knows us."

"I dunno," Brett answered absent-mindedly as he tried to swat a fly, "maybe he's planning to start a business and he's using us for practice."

Megan ignored that. "Do you know the story about his family?"

Brett thought about it. "I think our real estate agent mentioned something when we were first looking at the house. His marriage broke up a long time ago, and didn't Jim tell us a few weeks ago that he has a daughter about your age? Why do you ask?"

"No reason, it's just funny that he never talks about them, especially his daughter."

When they arrived at Jim's door, they were greeted with a smile and an offer of lemonade. Jim ushered them into his living room, where the roar of the air conditioner dominated the room.

He started off with a question. "Megan, I wanted to ask you. After everything we discussed last time, do you feel more comfortable now about investing in stocks?"

"Definitely," said Megan, "especially if we use the TDF approach and start to reduce our weighting in stocks as we get closer to retirement."

"Good," said Jim approvingly, "so you agree that stocks are much better than bonds over the long run?"

"Yes, but . . ."

Seeing Megan hesitate, Jim encouraged her to finish her thought, "Please go on."

"But that's not the same as saying that stocks are better than *any* other investment. Maybe they are, but I have no way of knowing."

Jim was curious now. "Which other type of investment were you thinking of?"

"Well, real estate? Like, maybe buying a condo and renting it out? We could make a steady income with the rent money coming in while the property appreciates in value. I heard a lot of people are doing that instead of investing in stocks. It seems that house prices are always going higher."

Jim nodded thoughtfully while he pondered how best to answer this. "You're absolutely right that many people prefer to invest in real estate. We shouldn't dismiss the idea without looking at some data first. I'm just not prepared to do that today; but tell you what, we will discuss real estate in the next session, after I've done some research. Deal?"

"Sounds good to me."

"As far as today is concerned," Jim said, "why don't we finish off on the question of investing in stocks?"

"I thought we already agreed on a TDF approach," Brett responded. "Was there something else on that subject that you wanted to cover?"

"There are some mini-strategies that I wanted to bring to your attention. They will lessen the risk of investing in stocks and might also improve your long-term performance. While I call them 'mini-strategies,' they can make a significant difference over the course of time. Shall we proceed?"

"By all means," said Megan with a smile. Brett joined in with a half-nod.

"Let me start with the more straightforward recommendations. First on the list is stock picking — don't do it, especially when it comes to speculative stocks. You'll get obsessed with checking up on your holdings several times a day, and you'll agonize over missed opportunities or poor performers."

"But if you get superior returns over time, doesn't that make it all worthwhile?" Brett challenged.

"That's a pretty big *if*," replied Jim. "For every story of someone who bought Amazon at $10 a share, there are a thousand untold stories of investors who did much worse than the benchmark indices. If you're patient, you'll get superior returns from buying and holding a basket of stocks for the long run and being well-diversified. There is just no reason to believe you can beat the market on a consistent basis by actively trading."

Brett was not easily deterred. "What if you had good inside information on a stock?"

"Trading on real inside information is illegal. As for what passes for inside information — so-called hot tips from friends or stockbrokers — that's a mug's game. Studies have shown the results are several percentage points *worse* than buying stocks at random."

Jim suddenly stopped when he saw Megan starting to smile. "What?" he asked.

"I love hearing old-fashioned expressions like 'mug's game,'" Megan declared happily. "That's the sort of thing my father used to say!"

Jim smiled back, but Brett ignored Megan's comment and asked, "If we don't pick our own stocks, what would we do instead?"

"Invest in a pool of stocks, something that is known as an equity fund. There are expensive ways of doing it via actively managed mutual funds, but I recommend you stay away from those. Just because something is expensive doesn't mean it's better; this is especially true with mutual funds, where most of the extra cost you pay represents sales commissions. Fortunately, there are also inexpensive ways to buy into an equity fund and your return should be just as good. I particularly like the idea of buying exchange-traded funds, better known as ETFs."

"I've heard of them," said Brett. "But aren't there hundreds of ETFs?"

"Yes, and it can be difficult to wade through all the possibilities without help. If you don't think you're up to it, then leave that job to someone else. For instance, you can sign up with a robo-advisor firm. They would charge you a fairly small ongoing fee to help you assess your risk tolerance and goals and choose an appropriate asset mix for you. They will then manage your portfolio on an ongoing basis in order to maintain the proper asset mix. Otherwise, you might drift away from your target mix as one asset class does better than another."

"How does that jibe with the TDF approach you just sold us on?" asked Brett.

"You don't actually need to buy TDFs to follow the TDF approach to setting asset mix. It just makes it easier. You can accomplish the same thing by buying ETFs and continually changing the asset mix yourself. This would entail reducing the stock weighting little by little — say, once every couple of years — while increasing the weighting in bonds. Which way you go depends on how comfortable you are with a DIY approach and how much you stand to save on fees."

Megan wondered aloud, "Either way, does a TDF approach eliminate our risk?"

"It eliminates some of it," replied Jim, "but by no means all. As we have previously discussed, stocks are inherently risky."

"Fair enough," said Megan. "Anything else we should know?"

"The second thing you should do is stay fully invested."

"I don't understand," said Brett. "Won't we always be fully invested in *something* as long as the money stays in the portfolio?"

"Let me be more specific," said Jim. "I'm saying don't try to time the market highs and lows. There will be times when the stock market will seem overheated and you're sure it's due for a fall. At times like that, you might be tempted to reduce your stock weighting with the hope of buying back later when stock prices drop. This type of behaviour is known as 'market timing.' It sounds great, but there is one major problem with it."

"Which is?"

"It doesn't work. It is one of the least successful investment strategies out there, and no respectable manager admits to engaging in market timing (even though all of them do it to a minor extent, they just call it something else). Many a stock market guru has made a name for himself (yes, it's usually a man) by correctly predicting a bear market, only to lose his reputation by being dead wrong the next time around.

"To summarize on this point, I suggest you stick with the asset mix dictated by the TDF approach and not deviate from it, ever. In this way, you'll develop a longer-term perspective on the market and won't get too fussed over short-term fluctuations."

As always, Brett was a little skeptical. "Surely there are times when the market is so overheated that you *know* it's due for a fall. And also times when it's so oversold after a market crash that you are sure you should be buying into it."

"You might think so," Jim responded, "but let me give you a little example of just how hard it is to time the market. Consider two investors, Stella and Audrey. Both of them have a fairly long-term investment horizon and both want to get the best return they can over a 20-year period. In my example, that period is 1996 to 2015.

"We'll start with Stella's experience. We will assume she is one of the most successful market timers of all time. At the beginning of 1996, Stella has $100,000 invested in a 60-40 portfolio. It does quite well for the first four years with an overall return of 62 percent, including dividends. By January 2000, Stella starts to worry that stocks are getting seriously overpriced. She sells off all her stocks and bonds and puts her money into safe government T-bills. The timing is great, as the dot-com bubble bursts just two and a half months later. She stays in T-bills throughout 2000 and 2001, both bad years to be in the market, and thereby avoids some serious losses. By January 2002, Stella gets back into the stock market. This turns out to be a tad early, but she still avoided most of the carnage. By 2003, investment returns surge back into positive territory and stay that way for several years.

"We now get to December 2005. By this point, the sub-prime lenders in the US mortgage market are making Stella nervous, so she repeats the exercise, selling off her 60-40 portfolio and going back into T-bills. She stays in T-bills for the entire period from 2006 to 2010. In the process, she is one of the few investors to survive the 2008–09 global market meltdown with all of her money intact. This time, Stella makes sure not to go back into stocks too early, so she waits until January 2011 to do so. After that, it is practically all blue skies as far as investments are concerned, so she enjoys good returns on her 60-40 portfolio from 2011 until 2015.

"Stella appears to be a success story. It is doubtful that any real-life investor, professional or otherwise, timed the market as well as Stella did during that 20-year stretch. Doing so would have required an exceptional level of prescience or luck. While she didn't get the market tops and bottoms right to the exact month, Stella still did very, very well.

"On the other hand, we have Audrey. Audrey took her $100,000 and invested it in a 60-40 asset mix starting in 1996. Unlike Stella, Audrey maintained this same 60-40 mix year in and year out until 2015. As a result, she suffered alongside all the other investors who lost money in 2001–02 and again in 2008–09."

At this point, Jim turned to Brett. "Who would you rather be in this story? Stella the prescient investor, or Audrey, the stodgy investor who plodded along and stayed fully invested at all times?"

Brett looked uncomfortable, "Based on the way you're asking, I know you want me to say Stella. Why don't you just give us the results?"

Jim took out a chart labelled Figure 13 and proceeded to describe what was going on. "This chart traces the growth in the portfolio for both Audrey and Stella. You'll note there was a brief time when Stella was ahead. That was in the midst of the 2008–09 financial meltdown. But Stella's lead dissolved very soon after the markets started to recover from that bear market. Even though Stella timed the two bear markets better than virtually any human being, Audrey's portfolio still outperformed Stella's in the longer term."

Figure 13: Even good market timing doesn't work

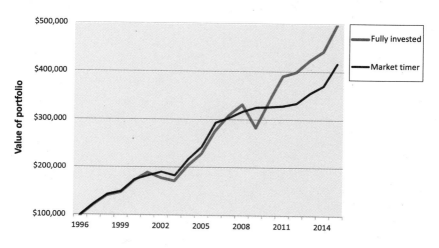

Brett looked deep in thought as he studied the chart. Finally, he said, "That's pretty amazing. Is there any chance the particular period you picked was an anomaly?"

"I don't think so," Jim replied. "I conducted a similar test over the years 1924 to 1940, a period that spanned the great market crash of 1929 and the Great Depression. Even with similarly very good (but not perfect) market timing, the person who stayed fully invested still ended up on top."

"How do you explain that?" asked Brett.

"Market timing ultimately fails because it is virtually impossible to sell at the very peak or buy at the very bottom. Doing so is important, since so much of the action in the stock market seems to occur in the last few months of one bull market and the first few months of the next. You don't want to miss either of those periods. Even if you are 98 percent correct like Stella was, it seems you are still going to be better off in the long run just staying fully invested. And if you're less than 98 percent correct, heaven help you."

Brett and Megan remained silent as they considered Jim's comments.

Megan spoke. "As always, Jim, we've learned something. Thank you so much. And next time?"

"We'll talk about investing in real estate," Jim promised.

Megan rubbed her hands with glee.

CHAPTER 11

Invest in Real Estate Instead of Stocks?

Saturday, July 23

During the following week, Jim was busy researching real estate returns and was scarcely seen outdoors. He was ready for Brett and Megan when they arrived on Saturday afternoon at the usual time.

"Welcome back, you two! Are you ready to talk about putting your retirement savings into real estate?"

"I've always been ready," declared Megan. "I just need you to tell me it's a good idea!"

"We'll find out today," Jim assured her. "As you pointed out last time, Megan, many people choose to buy a condo or two and rent them out. In the ideal situation, the rent they earn will be enough to cover the mortgage payments and various expenses. These include monthly maintenance fees, property taxes, commissions paid to agents and necessary upkeep. With luck and low mortgage rates, there might even be a little positive cash flow. Over time, they'll eventually pay off the mortgage on the condo, or maybe they sell it before that point. Either way, the hope is that they can eventually sell the condo for much more than they paid, with the proceeds being used to produce substantial retirement income."

"I like the sound of that," said Megan.

"That's the theory, anyway," Jim was careful to note. "It doesn't always work out. But I admit it has been a very profitable activity in major cities like Toronto and Vancouver for the past 20 years or so. The question is whether this sort of real estate play is a better way to invest your retirement savings than putting the money into stocks and bonds."

"I bet you're going to tell us it isn't," Brett declared.

"Actually, no," Jim replied. "I'm going to present you with some data and a couple of scenarios and let you come to your own conclusion. Scenario 1 is more optimistic than Scenario 2, though neither is at the extreme end of the spectrum. If you want to be mathematical about it, my scenarios would be positioned around the 20th percentile and the 80th percentile of all possible outcomes."[1]

Looking at his captive audience, Jim noticed a glazed look and made a mental note not to talk about percentiles again.

He continued to explain his approach to the problem, "Both scenarios will be based on the same initial circumstances. They will both involve buying a condo in an almost-new building in the city. Let's say the price of the condo is $400,000; you buy it by putting 20 percent down and securing the rest with a mortgage, which you amortize over 25 years. The first five years of the mortgage is based on an interest rate of 2.5 percent. Rather than trying to keep all these numbers in your head, I've put the details on my whiteboard."

Jim had clearly taken to the whiteboard that Brett and Megan had given him. He propped it up on the mantelpiece:

---

[1]   This means that Scenarios 1 and 2 are respectively better than all but 20 percent of outcomes and worse than 80 percent of outcomes.

Purchase price	$400,000
Down payment (20%)	$80,000
Mortgage payments[2]	$1,436/mo
Property taxes in year 1*	$300/yr
Monthly maintenance fee in year 1*	$250
What you can rent it for in year 1	$1,600/mo

*These increase with inflation.

"The numbers on the whiteboard are common to both scenarios," Jim explained. "First, we'll consider Scenario 1, the more optimistic of the two. Here is how I would describe it:

- You would be blessed with a series of mature, long-term tenants who each rent for five years; this minimizes 'down time' when you're not collecting any rent and also minimizes the number of times you have to pay commissions to real estate agents to find a new tenant.
- These model tenants always pay on time and never miss a payment.
- When you do need a new tenant, the condo is vacant for only a month and the cost to paint the place, sand and polish the floors, and do other minor repairs is fairly modest ($1,500 in present-day dollars).
- Inflation is a little higher than in recent years, with prices rising at 2.5 percent a year; this makes you feel even better about owning an asset that is traditionally a good hedge against inflation.
- You can increase the rent with inflation each year and also bump it up another 5 percent beyond inflation when a new tenant comes in, since we're assuming the rental market stays strong the entire time.
- Interest rates on mortgages stay low; initially, the rate is 2.5

---

2   First five years only. After that, it depends on the direction of interest rates.

percent and increases to 3 percent after five years, which is where it stays for the rest of the time you own the condo.

- Most important of all, house prices in the city rise by a very robust 3.5 percent a year in real terms, and they manage to do this every year that you own the property. To put this into perspective, this rate of increase is greater than you would have found almost anywhere else in the world.

- Your particular condo also rises in price by 3.5 percent a year in real terms (6 percent in nominal terms), less 0.5 percent annual depreciation."

Megan reacted to the last point, "Whoa, what is the depreciation all about? I thought real estate tended to appreciate, not depreciate."

"The housing market as a whole is definitely appreciating in value, which is why I have prices going up in real terms by 3.5 percent a year. But any one unit gradually ages compared to the rest of the market. The unit you own becomes a tiny bit less attractive year by year in relative terms. It will still appreciate, mind you, just not as much as the market as a whole."

Megan didn't seem convinced, so Jim tried again.

"Look at it this way. All things being equal, buyers and renters prefer a brand-new space rather than one in an older building, even if it has been renovated. Part of this desire is rational, since newer buildings may have features that are absent in older buildings and are less likely to have things break down. Besides, it's just human nature to prefer new things over used. If two units were available that were somehow identical in space, layout and amenities, but one was brand new and the other was 20 years old, would you be surprised to learn that the older one was selling for 10 percent less?"

Megan relented. "I guess not."

Jim paused to let his listeners absorb the situation he had described, then he asked, "Would you therefore both agree that seeing your investment property rising 3 percent a year faster than inflation would be an excellent outcome?"

"Yes, but how did you get to 3 percent?" asked Megan.

"It's the 3.5 percent I mentioned earlier less the 0.5 percent depreciation on any one given property as it ages relative to the market."

Brett had a question. "I thought house prices were going up even faster than that, at least in cities like Toronto."

"They were for a while," said Jim. "According to *The Economist*, house prices in Toronto rose in real terms by 4.6 percent a year between 2001 and 2020. Going forward, that rate of increase isn't sustainable as Toronto housing closes in on the prices in other world-class cities. In New York, for instance, the average real increase in prices was just 1.9 percent a year over the same period. In fact, during the COVID-19 pandemic, condo prices temporarily fell double digits in Toronto. My assumption of a 3.5 percent real increase for another 20 years is actually quite aggressive when you consider what the market has already done and what is happening elsewhere. I don't think you could assume any more than that without bringing a housing bubble into the picture."

Brett had no more to say on the subject, so Jim moved on. "If you're going to invest in condos, though, you can't do it immediately. You'll have to wait a while, maybe five to ten years."

"Why is that?" asked Megan.

"You don't have the cash now. You only just recently bought the home you live in, which consumed all the capital you had and saddled you with a hefty mortgage. Moreover, you have practically nothing set aside yet for retirement. To buy the condo in my example, you will need to make a down payment of $80,000, which will take you years to accumulate, especially because it is after-tax money."

"You're saying we can't buy a rental property through our RRSP?" asked Brett.

"I'm afraid not," answered Jim. "An RRSP can't hold real estate. It could hold the mortgage on the condo, but that doesn't help you in this situation. If we want to think about an immediate investment, let's do something else. Brett, you mentioned you had an older cousin named Jeff. I believe you said he was 42? It would be more realistic to use him in our example.

"Let's assume that Jeff and his wife, Sandra, have been contributing to a TFSA over the past 10 years and their combined TFSA balance is now $80,000. It is Jeff and Sandra who buy the condo to rent out, and they will be the beneficiaries of the best-case scenario I've just described."

Megan was a little disappointed that someone else was buying her condo but stayed quiet.

"We'll assume they buy the condo and hold onto it for 20 years before selling it. Because of the mortgage payments and the various expenses and taxes, their cash flow is negative for the first 15 years. In other words, they are still pumping new money into their investment for the first 15 years, but they don't really mind, since the property is appreciating in value."

Nods from both Brett and Megan.

"Even though their cash flow is negative, they still have to pay income tax every year. That is because they can't recognize the full mortgage payments as an expense for tax purposes, only the *interest* portion of the mortgage expenses."

Nods again, though a little slower than last time.

"Anyway," Jim continued, "time passes, and after 20 years, they sell the condo for a handsome profit. The proceeds after paying off the residual mortgage debt, and after commissions and the capital gains tax on the sale, are $742,000. These are after-tax dollars that they can use to help fund their retirement."

Jim wiped the whiteboard clean and wrote that number down on a table he had started. Brett and Megan weren't sure what to make yet of this example, but the first number sounded impressive.

As if Jim were reading their minds, he went on to say, "I'll put this figure into context. We can only tell how good this result is by comparing it to how well your cousin Jeff would have made out in stocks and bonds instead. Let's assume that they left the initial $80,000 in their TFSA and invested it in a 60-40 asset mix. Let's also assume that they deposited additional amounts each year into the TFSA. Each deposit is equal to the negative cash flow that the condo investment produced."[3]

"Essentially, you're saying it's apples and apples," Brett surmised, "including the tax impact. What's the result?"

"In a similarly best-case scenario for stocks and bonds," Jim replied, "their TFSA would have been worth $630,000 after 20 years."

Jim wrote this number down on the whiteboard as well and displayed the growing table to Brett and Megan.

---

3 And to be consistent, they took money out of the TFSA in the latter years to coincide with the years when the cash flow on the condo investment turned positive.

	Scenario 1	Scenario 2
Condo option	$742,000	
TFSA option (stocks & bonds)	$630,000	

Megan whistled in delight. "I knew it! It's better to invest in real estate after all!"

Jim nodded and said, "It *does* look pretty good, doesn't it? If you could rely on such an optimistic scenario materializing, you would never have to worry about stocks and bonds again. But we're not done yet."

Before Jim could go on, Brett wanted to be sure he had enough information to vet the example. He asked, "Will you give us the details behind your calculations, just so we have them?"

"Certainly," said Jim. "I'll print it all out for you at the end of this session.[4] The trouble is, you can't count on having a best-case scenario. A lot of things had to go right to be able to achieve the result I'm showing on the whiteboard. Now, let's move on to Scenario 2. It's more pessimistic, but equally plausible. It is just as likely to happen as Scenario 1. Consider it the flip side of the coin.

"In Scenario 2, I will assume the following:

- You have fair-to-middling experience with renters; their average stay in the condo is just two years rather than five, but at least they are still paying their rent and doing so on time.
- When you do need to rent it out again, the condo is vacant for two months until you can get someone else in there instead of just one; and each time, some improvements have to be made to attract a new tenant (same cost as Scenario 1, just incurred more often).
- Inflation rises by 2 percent a year rather than 2.5 percent.
- You can still increase the rent in line with inflation each year, but the housing market is not quite robust enough to be able to bump up the rent an extra 5 percent each time there is a new tenant.

---

4   This is shown at the end of this chapter.

- The annual budget for repairs is a little higher than under the best-case scenario but is still not too punishing.
- Interest rates on mortgages start at 2.5 percent again but ultimately rise to 5 percent; this is nothing like the bad old days, but it's definitely higher than homeowners have seen in recent years.
- The property appreciates in real terms by 0.5 percent a year (which becomes nil after offsetting it by the depreciation I mentioned earlier)."

Brett commented, "I have to say that none of this sounds all that bad. It's actually pretty close to what I would have assumed anyway. How did you come up with your estimate for the appreciation in the value of the condo under this scenario?"

"It's based on historical data," explained Jim. "The approximate annual increase in the real value of house prices in Canada between 1938 and 2001 was 0.4 percent.[5] For this scenario, I generously rounded it up to 0.5 percent."

"Why didn't you use the entire period, 1938 to 2019?"

"I used data only for the years up to 2001 because I was trying to create a slightly pessimistic scenario, but one that could still be justified historically. And I think we accomplish that by basing the assumption on the average increase in house prices over a 64-year period."

Silence ensued. Jim broke it by adding, "It could be worse, you know. I hear of people who bought condos in Florida and ended up selling them many years later for just about the same price as they paid, which means they would have suffered a big loss in real terms. At least in this scenario, the property is still rising with inflation every year."

Megan was barely listening to Jim at this point, since she was anxiously awaiting the result. "So, when you do your magic under Scenario 2, what do you get?"

---

5   This housing data comes from two sources: For the years from 1975 and on, from the International House Price Database maintained by the Federal Reserve Bank of Dallas. For earlier years, from a paper in the *American Economic Review* called "No Price Like Home: Global House Prices, 1870–2012."

Jim wordlessly consulted his spreadsheet and proceeded to complete the table on the whiteboard:

	Scenario 1	Scenario 2
Condo option	$742,000	$241,000
TFSA option (stocks & bonds)	$630,000	$430,000

Brett and Megan had trouble getting their minds around these new numbers.

"Seriously, Jim," exclaimed Megan. "That just can't be. The condo option under Scenario 2 provides barely a third as much money as under Scenario 1, and yet it didn't seem like your forecast was that much worse."

"It wasn't," Jim confirmed. "This example shows how a fairly small change in circumstances can produce a huge change in outcome when you invest in real estate."

"But why?" Megan persisted. "I feel I'm missing something."

Jim reflected on that for a moment before answering. "Basically, it's about leverage. For the 20 years that Jeff is paying off the mortgage on this condo, he never fully owns the place. In the first year, he would own only 20 percent of it with the rest being debt. A high debt-to-equity ratio is wonderful when an investment is rising in value, because it amplifies your return. Leverage, however, is a two-edged sword. If you catch the markets on the downside — and believe me, things can get much worse than Scenario 2 — you can lose your entire investment."

"It's rather ironic," Megan mused. "I asked you to check out real estate for us because I was worried there was too much risk in the stock market. But from what you're saying, we'd be jumping from the frying pan . . ."

Brett finished her thought: ". . . into the fire."

Jim nodded. "In recent years, we have already seen the markets starting to run into headwinds. It started in Vancouver a few years ago when they imposed special taxes to cool the housing market. Then, with the pandemic, owning real estate has become more problematic elsewhere. As I said earlier, in Toronto, condo prices briefly fell double digits in 2020. It is still a far cry from the collapse in housing prices that occurred between 1989 and 2000 in both Vancouver and Toronto, which means we haven't necessarily seen the worst yet. If you're going to invest in condos, you have to hope something like that never happens again, but there are no guarantees.

"It's not just the ending value that can make you think twice about becoming a landlord. Cash flow can be a problem, too. You may face an unexpected expense like having to buy a new refrigerator. Even an expense that you expected, like property tax coming due, might come at an inconvenient time. If the place is vacant for a while, or if the tenant simply can't pay for a couple of months, it means no rental income, just expenses; these things can easily happen."

Megan sighed. "I guess you're telling me that if it were you, you would never invest in real estate."

"Actually, I might," said Jim, "under the right conditions. For example, if I was in a high-income bracket and had maxed out on my contributions to RRSPs and TFSAs, but I still wanted to invest more, real estate might be the way to do it. It's more tax-effective than some types of investment. Also, it would be a good way to take advantage of low interest rates. Finally, the results could be very good, as we saw in the example. If I had enough money stashed away already in tax-assisted vehicles, I could afford to take the risk." Then he stopped and stared off into space for a moment.

"On second thought, I probably wouldn't," Jim corrected himself. "The opportunity for gain is certainly there, but not everything is about money. Being a landlord involves a lot of unexpected work. Every non-functioning appliance, sticking door, blocked drain and dripping faucet is your responsibility. Heaven help you if the apartment floods at three o'clock in the morning.

"Moreover, you'll find that tenants have higher expectations for a home they rent than a home they own; you can't let things slide the way you could in your own place. Renters think they are paying for everything to work perfectly and, legally, you're on the hook. So, if you don't live nearby, or if you aren't handy, it becomes both expensive and time-consuming dealing with the trades for repairs."

"Wow," said Megan. "It's starting to make me wonder why anyone goes through the hassle of investing in real estate."

"I guess it's a beautiful thing to see an investment property soar in value," Jim offered. "As I said, leverage is great when it works in your favour. We've seen years — at least in Vancouver and Toronto — where properties weren't rising by just 5 percent but more like 10 or 20 percent; that has to be part of the attraction. You just shouldn't try to talk yourself into thinking that this is normal or that residential real estate prices can't go down.

"Ultimately, you should do what you are most comfortable doing. For the purposes of our ongoing retirement planning exercise, though, I'm going to continue to assume you invest in stocks and bonds, specifically using the TDF approach." Then Jim gave them a wink and said, "One of you will have to break the bad news to Jeff."

Another thought came to Brett. "It seems that a lot of the risk in real estate investing has to do with leverage; owning just a small piece of the investment with the rest being debt. Don't we have the same problem with owning our house?"

Jim's eyes lit up. "That's very interesting you raise that question, Brett. It's not normally seen as a problem because no one thinks the price of homes will ever go down, but it was certainly a big problem in the US starting in 2007. Canada shouldn't consider itself to be immune. In general, home-owning has been a good long-term option in this country since at least World War II, but it doesn't mean things can't change. Would you like to analyze whether it's better to rent or to own?"

Brett looked at Megan and answered, "Sure, why not?"

"Okay," said Jim. "I think we can tackle that next week. The usual time."

Not for the first time, Brett and Megan went home with many thoughts swirling in their heads.

A bit more about . . .

Table 9: Assumptions that Jim used for the real estate example

	Best-case scenario	Worst-case scenario
Price appreciation on the condo* (real)	3.0%	0.5%
Return on alternative TFSA investments (real, net of fees)**	5.5%	2.0%
Price inflation	2.5%	2.0%

Marginal tax rate for purposes of cash flow and proceeds on sale (half of capital gain affected)	40%	40%
Annual rent increases	2.5%	2.0%
Additional one-time rent increase with new tenant	5.0%	0%
Mortgage interest rate — first 5 years	2.5%	2.5%
Mortgage interest rate — second 5 years	3.0%	3.0%
Mortgage interest rate — after 10 years	3.0%	5.0%
Annual cost of repairs (today's dollars)	$600	$900
Cost of minor renovations between tenants (today's dollars)	$1,500	$1,500
When cash flow on condo investment turns positive	Year 16	Never
Commissions paid to find a new tenant	1-month rent	1-month rent
Commissions paid on sale of property	5.0%	5.0%

*Net of 0.5% annual depreciation due to aging.

**These were set at about the 80th and 20th percentiles of all possible returns on a 60-40 asset mix.

CHAPTER 12

Is It Better to Rent or to Own?

Saturday, July 30

Just before they headed to Jim's place the following Saturday for their regular session, Megan had something she wanted to tell Brett.

"I was talking to Jim's next-door neighbour on the other side — you know, Mrs. Gladstone. She said Jim has been living alone for many years. And she can't remember the last time she saw Jim's daughter."

"Hmm, maybe Jim had a nasty divorce and the daughter got caught in the middle," Brett mused. "But don't you think it's better if we didn't poke our nose in his affairs?"

Megan clearly didn't think so, but she said nothing. She wasn't about to let this drop but knew this wasn't the time to pursue it.

When they arrived at Jim's place and sat down in his living room, Jim introduced the topic of the day. "Last time we spoke, we raised the idea of renting. This subject isn't about retirement-planning in the normal sense, but believe me, deciding whether to rent or to own your home can make a huge difference in how ready you'll be for retirement."

"Isn't the answer going to be obvious?" asked Brett. "It must be better to own than to rent."

Jim smiled. "Mark Twain once said, 'What gets us into trouble is not what we don't know. It's what we know for sure that just ain't so.' Let's see if this subject falls into that category.

"What we do know is that almost every working Canadian eventually wants to own a home. The national home ownership rate is over 66 percent; and if you take people under 30 out of the equation, as well as the bottom 30 percent of income-earners, the ownership rate rises to 90 percent. Can so many people be wrong? You wouldn't think so, but the fact is, owning has not always been better than renting. At least not financially."

"I'm surprised to hear that," said Brett.

Jim responded, "The even bigger surprise is that renting has been a better choice when you would least expect it — in the last 10 years."

"You can't be serious," Brett replied. "The housing market has been red hot during that time."

"I know, but so have stocks," said Jim. "We will use my spreadsheet to see what would have happened over each 30-year period, starting with 1938 to 1967. In the homeowner scenario, I will assume you buy the most home you can afford with mortgage payments equal to 22 percent[1] of gross pay in the first year, plus a down payment equal to $80,000 in today's dollars but deflated by the change in national average wages over that time. Your combined earnings in today's dollars are $110,000, but we deflate that, too, as we go back in time. For instance, if the first year of the 30-year period was 1990, you would have bought a home worth $147,000 at the time, with a down payment of $38,000.

"In the renter scenario, I assume you would invest an amount equal to the cash flow in the homeowner scenario. For instance, if you were renting for the first time in 1990, you would have invested $38,000 plus an amount equal to the homeowner's mortgage payments less the net amount paid on renting an equivalent home.[2] To the extent you had capital gains or losses

---

1   Nothing magical about 22 percent. This seemed to be a reasonable, albeit arbitrary, percentage.

2   Details are given at the end of the chapter.

on your investments, I assumed you would pay the appropriate income tax annually. To make it an apples-to-apples comparison, I made allowances for the property taxes, insurance and home maintenance that you would have to pay as a homeowner but not as a renter. For instance, if those three components added up to $6,000 in a given year, I assumed that you, the renter, would be investing that amount of money, too."

"Er, this is getting a little complicated, Jim," Brett interrupted. "I'm sure we can trust you on the methodology. Apples-to-apples, right?"

"I'm just trying to show you that I took some pains to ensure this was a fair comparison and that there was some science behind it."

"Really, Jim, was there ever any doubt?" Megan commented with a wink.

Jim kept going, "When we put it all together, I can show how much wealth one would have accumulated at the end of each 30-year period as a homeowner and as a renter." He handed out a chart to illustrate.

Figure 14: Owning versus renting — wealth after 30 years

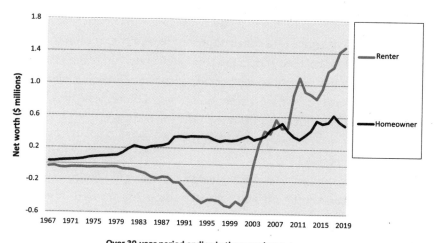

Over 30-year period ending in the year shown

Anyone retiring after 2009 would have been better off renting for their entire working lives.

House prices sources: International House Price Database (Federal Reserve Bank of Dallas) and the paper "No Price Like Home: Global House Prices 1870–2012" (*American Economic Review*).

"As the chart shows, homeowners would have enjoyed a much higher net worth than renters in periods ending before 2001. In fact, the renter's net worth was actually negative for periods ending in the 1990s. This is more or less what we expect to see."

"Wow, renters would have got clobbered back then!" Brett exclaimed. "What was going on, exactly?"

"Take the 30-year periods that ended in the 1990s," Jim explained. "Monthly rent in the latter years would have been higher than making mortgage payments on a property bought many years earlier. Let's take the low point, which is the 30-year period ending in 1999. The renter's net worth would have been negative $530,000, while for the homeowner it was a positive $300,000. The main reason the homeowner did so much better during this period is explained by one word: inflation. The house value rose over seven-fold since the beginning of the period; the renter would obviously have missed out on that.

"Also, renters at the time were paying a lot more in rent relative to the house price than they are today. I've estimated the annual rent to be 7 percent of the price of a home in the 1970s and the first half of the 1980s. It started to decline a little after that, but the ratio was still in the high sixes by 1999. By comparison, renters today are paying annual rent that is closer to 4 percent of the price of a comparable home. Another reason that renters did so badly is because mortgage payments ended up being much less than rent just a few years into the period. Even if interest rates were fairly high then, mortgage payments were on the low side because they largely reflect the low cost of the home at the start of the period."

"Okay, that makes sense," said Megan, "but I am shocked to see how it flips around after 2009."

"You mean the fact that the homeowner advantage disappears? This happened because inflation was low after 2009 and so were rents relative to home price. This is the opposite of the conditions that prevailed before 2000."

Brett was skeptical. "It's hard to believe that you wouldn't be better off owning a home at least in Toronto and Vancouver!"

"You have a point, Brett," replied Jim. "This analysis is based on home price increases for a composite of Canadian cities. Homeowners in Toronto or Vancouver would have fared somewhat better. For instance, the index I used indicates house prices rose by 4.2 percent a year in real terms since 2000, whereas *The Economist* reports that Toronto prices have gone up by 4.6 percent a year. That extra 0.4 percent a year, compounded, makes a difference.

"On the other hand, as I mentioned last time, what has been happening in the Toronto and Vancouver housing markets literally cannot go on forever. Home prices in these cities might remain high, but future *increases* in those prices will eventually moderate."

"What are you suggesting, then?" asked Megan, who was now looking a little distraught. "That we should sell our house and rent a place instead?"

Jim knew he had to tread gently. "There are many reasons why people want to own a home, and some of the most important reasons have nothing to do with money. You have more choice if you own instead of rent. You can make whatever improvements to the property you want (assuming Brett goes along with them). Owning also provides stability, which isn't always possible if you rent. These are all good reasons to own."

Jim's words mollified Megan, so he felt it safe to return to the numbers. "As for financial considerations, what I like about owning is that the increase in wealth is relatively stable. You can see that in the chart. By renting, you might hit a home run, but you couldn't afford to encounter a scenario like 1970 to 1999 when you would have had so much less wealth going into retirement."

"Bottom line, Jim?" asked Brett.

"You don't want to take undue risk with your retirement, and renting substantially increases your risk of a really bad outcome. As far as the future is concerned, we can take one final look at this question of renting versus buying." Then, glancing at Megan, Jim added, "We'll do that just to satisfy our intellectual curiosity. You have enough on your hands to ensure you save properly for retirement without thinking about moving. The thing is, we can't have that discussion immediately, since we need to lay the groundwork first. This involves mapping out our long-term forecast for the capital markets and inflation."

"Great," said Brett. "Is that what we're going to talk about next time? The future?"

"Not yet," said Jim. "Before we get there, I would like to introduce one more enhancement to your saving strategy!"

Brett seemed to have enjoyed the session, but Megan didn't want to hear any more about renting.

A bit more about . . . Other Assumptions Underlying the Comparison of Renting versus Buying

Data on historic house prices	For prices from 1975 and later, the International House Price Database kept by the Federal Reserve Bank of Dallas. For pre-1975 prices, the paper "No Price Like Home: Global House Prices 1870–2012," in the *American Economic Review,* vol. 107, no. 2 (February 2017).
Marginal income tax rate on stock market gains	40% rate, which means income tax of 20% on a capital gain.
Composition of stock portfolio	50% in S&P/TSX index and 50% in S&P 500 (converted to Canadian dollars); MER 60 bps.
Ongoing cost of owning	Estimated at 1.25% of current market value of the home to cover property tax, insurance and maintenance fees.
Historic mortgage interest rates	Estimated from yields on three- to five-year Government of Canada bonds plus 1.5%, then rounded; five-year closed fixed mortgages are assumed.

CHAPTER 13

One More Enhancement

Saturday, August 6

Even though it was a long weekend, the next session took place the following Saturday at the usual afternoon time.

Jim told them, "I hope we've got real estate out of our system so we can get back to saving basics. We've covered a lot of ground in the last few weeks and it's easy to get lost in the details. Why don't we take a high-level view of what we've done before we go any further?"

Since there were no objections, Jim walked over to his cherished whiteboard. Flourishing a marker, he asked, "Who would like to start?"

Over the course of the next 20 minutes, the three of them rehashed all the topics they had covered in the last few weeks. The following is an expanded version of what Jim ultimately wrote down on the whiteboard:[1]

---

[1]   While each bullet point was summarized with only a few key words on the whiteboard, this fleshed-out summary gives a better idea of the conversation that accompanied it.

- Saving a flat 10 percent of pay a year may not be enough to retire well.
- Saving 12 percent is *probably* closer to the recommended saving rate, at least for Brett and Megan, since they have 30 years to save and don't plan to retire too early.
- Saving that much isn't always possible in the early years due to high expenses (e.g., daycare, mortgage payments).
- The Rule of 30 makes saving less painful without compromising the primary goal of saving enough.
- One should save based on the Rule of 30, at least until age 50 or 55. After that, it is better to use a retirement income calculation tool, like PERC, to fine-tune one's saving rate.
- Plan for the vulnerable years, the time late in a career when you might be forced out of your regular job by your employer or by a health issue; in particular, pay off the mortgage a few years early, just in case.
- Use a target-date-fund (TDF) approach to setting asset mix rather than a constant 60-40.
- Stay fully invested at all times; don't try to time the market with sudden changes in asset mix.
- From a retirement planning perspective, owning your own home is safer than renting, though the financial advantage of owning isn't what it used to be.

Jim stared at the whiteboard. "If we accept all that, let's redo the savings projection showing spendable income before and after retirement. We will ignore the possible drop in earnings during the vulnerable years because we covered that previously, but we'll make use of everything else that I've listed on the whiteboard. In other words, we'll do the following:

- assume once again that you experience the same inflation and investment returns as during the worst 30-year period in history (1946 to 1975),
- save using the Rule of 30 during this period,
- trade up to a new home after 10 years,

- apply the TDF approach to setting your asset mix and
- optimize your retirement income using the ideas from *Retirement Income for Life*."

"In addition to all that," Jim announced, "we'll do one more thing to make this projection even better."

"Sounds exciting!" Megan exclaimed. "What is it?"

"Not exciting at all, really. It is something we've talked about but haven't put into action, until now. We will use PERC to recalculate your saving rate when you're five years away from retirement."

"Why five?" asked Brett.

"It could have been 10 years," Jim conceded. "But in the case of our projection, you would have kept on contributing based on the Rule of 30 until five years before retirement anyway. At that point your mortgage is paid off, after which your spendable income soars. That is when you have to make the critical decision to regulate your spendable income."

"You're losing me," Brett warned.

Jim tried again. "At the point the mortgage is paid off, you might say to yourself, 'Okay, we can enjoy much higher spendable income for the next five years until we retire and then take a big cut in spendable income as we go into retirement.' The shock of that spending drop might be more than you're willing to bear, though, so instead you contribute an additional 10 percent of pay to an RRSP for your last five working years."

Brett was doing the math in his head. "In those last five years, the Rule of 30 already has us contributing 30 percent of pay to retirement saving. You're saying bump it up another 10 percent?"

"That's right."

"Isn't that crazy? Saving 40 percent?"

"What's crazy is saving for retirement when you are already having trouble making ends meet," Jim retorted. "I know that saving 40 percent of pay sounds like a lot, but you would still have enough spendable income to produce the highest standard of living of your career. More important, the extra saving means you can more or less carry that higher spendable income into your retirement years."

Megan looked a little dubious. "Jim, do you have a chart to show how this would look?"

Figure 15: Closing the income gap by saving more in later working years

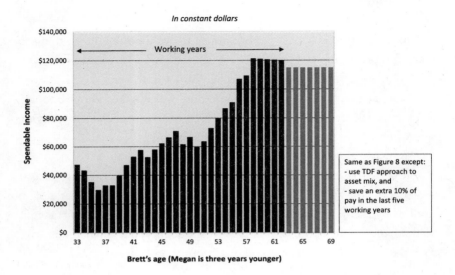

In constant dollars

Working years

Spendable income

Same as Figure 8 except:
- use TDF approach to asset mix, and
- save an extra 10% of pay in the last five working years

Brett's age (Megan is three years younger)

"As a matter of fact, I do," Jim replied. "I prepared it before you came today." He handed out the new page.

"Wow!" Brett and Megan said in unison before Megan continued, "This is looking really good now. Except for a small dip in our 30s and again around 50, our spendable income is rising throughout our working years, just like we wanted. But I see that our spendable income in retirement is still slightly lower than in our last five working years."

"True," Jim conceded, "but higher than at any other point in your life. I could have closed that little gap by upping your saving rate to 41 or 42 percent instead of 40 percent, but that's just fine-tuning."

Brett was rubbing his chin. "Is there any way we could have achieved the same spendable income in retirement without having to contribute 40 percent of pay in those last five years?"

"There are two ways, actually. One of them is dumb, which is to save even more in your early years when you're barely scraping by on spendable income that is just a fraction of what it will become when you're closer to retirement."

Brett and Megan had already heard this refrain, so they waited for Jim to continue.

"But there is another way to boost your retirement income a little without saving more — a good way. It involves tapping into the one other major source of wealth you have, other than your retirement savings."

"Which is . . . ?" quizzed Megan.

"I'll let you figure it out," Jim answered, a little cryptically. "I'll give you a hint: What else do you have that is of significant value and easily sold?"

Brett and Megan looked deep in thought for a few seconds when Megan suddenly exclaimed, "Oh! You mean our house, don't you?"

"Precisely," said Jim.

"But we need a place to live!" Brett objected.

"Of course you do," said Jim. "I'm not talking about doing anything extreme. I'm just saying that you could downsize your home around the time of retirement to free up maybe 20 percent of the equity in your home. That amount would be enough to close the gap in spendable income that I showed in Figure 15. You could then use the other 80 percent of the equity to buy a smaller place, perhaps a condo, or move out of the city entirely. But you wouldn't take such a major step just to boost your retirement income by just a few thousand dollars each year. It's the kind of action you would reserve for a crisis situation."

"How do you define a crisis situation?" asked Megan.

"If you faced the perfect storm," Jim replied. "For instance, if you lost your job a few years before retirement and also faced a prolonged downturn in the stock market, as actually happened toward the end of 1946–75 period. Those are rather grim circumstances, but it is nice to know you could survive them and head into retirement in pretty good financial shape."

Jim continued, "Of course, not everyone downsizes for financial reasons. You might want to do so for a change in lifestyle, like moving into a condo so you wouldn't have to worry about yard work anymore or because you want to enjoy living in the city. I know a lot of affluent couples who have downsized."

"I guess that's reasonable," said Megan, frowning as she glanced over at Brett. "Though I'd prefer to have the option of staying in the same house when I retire."

"That's doable, too," said Jim. "Instead of downsizing, the other thing you could do to boost your income is to take out a reverse mortgage."

"A reverse mortgage?" Brett echoed.

"Yes," said Jim. "It's a way to borrow against the equity in your home without having to pay it back, at least not in your lifetime. There aren't many institutions in Canada that provide this service, but there are some. The institutional lender would give you a lump sum, or better still, a series of payments over a period like 10 or 15 years. The loan does eventually have to get repaid, of course, but not as long as one of you is still alive and still living in the same place. It's only after you both die or sell the house that the bank would recoup the money you owe them."

"What's the catch?" Brett persisted.

"The 'catch,' if you will, is that the interest they charge for a reverse mortgage is a little higher than the interest you would normally pay on a first mortgage or a home equity loan. Also, if you ever decide to move, you would have to repay the loan immediately, which might not be convenient. For that reason, you probably shouldn't think about getting a reverse mortgage until you're 75 or so, by which time you ought to have a good idea of whether you'll ever want to move again."

"I guess it's something to consider," said Brett, as he started to stretch. "Would you recommend it?"

"If you were 75 and needed income, the answer is yes. The good news is that you don't have to worry about this issue for a good 40 years yet, and maybe never.[2] In the meantime, it is enough to know that there is a solution other than downsizing in case you find you didn't save quite enough."

Brett concurred, "It's nice to know we have an ace up our sleeve, but I'm glad we don't have to think about playing that card for a long time to come."

Megan said, "This has been amazing, Jim. It looks like you have an answer to all the nasty things that could sabotage our retirement saving, like bad investment returns and lost income. We can't thank you enough."

---

2   For readers who want to know more about how this option might affect your decumulation strategy, this is Enhancement 5 in *Retirement Income for Life*.

"Not so fast!" Jim exclaimed. "I didn't say we were finished! So far, we have focussed on the past, but we still need to think about the future. Will it be just a repeat of some past period or something entirely different?"

"I take it that's a rhetorical question," said Megan, smiling. "By the way, do you have plans tomorrow night or can you join us for a barbecue? I think we should celebrate this milestone, and what better time than on a long weekend?"

Jim happily accepted.

CHAPTER 14

A Final Look at the Past

Sunday, August 7

Jim went over to Brett and Megan's backyard the following evening, armed with a six-pack of Heineken and a mysterious folder.

Brett decided not to ask. He popped the caps off a couple of bottles and handed one to Jim. "I don't know what else you plan to throw at us, Jim, but I really think we're getting our hands around this retirement saving problem."

Jim held up his beer in salute, "Thanks, Brett. I've enjoyed these weekly sessions. As I mentioned, we're nearly finished the historical part of the analysis. There is just one more thing I wanted to show you before we move on."

Megan, who was just coming out of the house with plates and cutlery, overheard the last part of the conversation. "Good evening, Jim. What are you guys talking about?"

"Hi, Megan. Since this evening is a sort of celebration, I thought we should take a look at a more typical historic scenario before we move on. Something you can hope for instead of fear."

"I thought you weren't going to work tonight," said Megan, smiling.

"I don't see these projections as work," Jim replied. "And besides, the chart that I'm about to show you is something I printed off earlier today."

In the meantime, Brett went back inside to bring out the salmon for the barbecue.

Megan took this as her opportunity to ask a personal question. "Jim, does your daughter live in the city?"

Jim stiffened slightly at the mention of his daughter. "Yes, but we don't see each other. Alyssa blamed me for leaving her mother."

"Wasn't that a long time ago, though?"

"Yes, but . . ."

At that point, Brett had rejoined them in the backyard. Jim wasn't in a mood to carry on this conversation, and Megan knew well enough not to insist.

Jim quickly changed the subject. "As I was saying, we can learn something from the past, not only the bad times but also the good. So far, we have been using the investment returns from the period 1946 to 1975 to determine your saving rate. That happened to be the worst 30-year period since the 1930s to invest in."

"Now you're going to show us the best 30-year period?" asked Brett hopefully.

"Well, no, there's no point. I don't want to lull you into a sense of false security with a scenario that is unlikely to materialize and that, frankly, is one you don't need. Instead, I was thinking we'd take a look at the *average* 30-year period. I used the word 'average' a little loosely. I really mean the period that produced the median real return over all 30-year periods; better than half the periods and worse than the other half."

"When was that?" asked Brett as he scraped the hot barbecue grill.

"From 1938 to 1967," Jim replied. "The average real return over those 30 years was 5.0 percent based on the 60-40 asset mix. That's a lot better than the 2.6 percent return for the 1946–75 period, but it's still just the median. And if you use the TDF approach to asset mix, you would have done even better with an average real return of 6.2 percent."

"And that's just a typical historical period?" Brett asked, incredulous.

"The good old days!" replied Jim with a smile. "Note that in the 1938–67 period, the inflation rate and bond yields were somewhat similar to what we have been seeing in recent years and what I expect we will continue to see for quite some time to come. The average inflation rate over the entire 30 years was 2.9 percent. As for long-term bonds, the yield at the start of the period was in the 3 percent range, which may be high by today's standards but is low, historically. The yield then slowly climbed to 6 percent by the end of the period. We won't necessarily see the same trajectory over the next 30 years, but it's not out of the question."

"Exactly why are we looking at this scenario?" asked Megan as she set the patio table for dinner.

"I wanted you to see what 'normal' looks like, or at least what it used to look like," said Jim. "We actuaries tend to be a gloomy bunch. We embrace pessimism a little too easily, so this might provide a bit of a reality check later on, when we start to make long-term forecasts. Also, I want you to see how well the Rule of 30 works under a more typical historic scenario." Jim handed out a chart to illustrate.

"It looks sort of like the last chart, Figure 15," Brett observed.

"Yes, except that spendable income is now considerably higher," Jim replied. "Your spendable income in retirement is $144,000 under this

Figure 16: Result in a more typical historical period

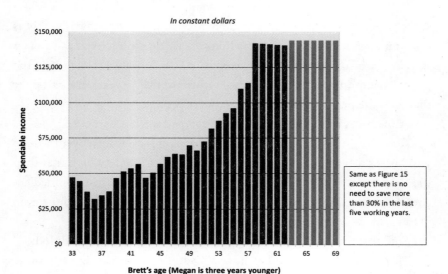

In constant dollars

Spendable income

Same as Figure 15 except there is no need to save more than 30% in the last five working years.

Brett's age (Megan is three years younger)

scenario, and that's in today's dollars. That is more than triple your current spendable income, which I estimated to be $46,000 and which will go down further once kids arrive. What this chart shows is how well you could have done in a typical past period had you followed the Rule of 30 and all the other tips we've talked about so far."

Brett wanted a clarification. "But you're not saying we can expect the future to match the typical past period?"

"No, I'm not," Jim confirmed, "but it's nice to know that it's at least possible."

As Brett and Megan kept staring at the chart, Jim took a sniff and asked, "Brett, are you watching the barbecue?"

PART II

Why the Future Will Be Different

CHAPTER 15

Pondering the Unknowable

Saturday, August 13

There were storm clouds threatening the following Saturday afternoon, so they took their session inside to their usual spot — Jim's living room beside the whiteboard.

"I hope you're getting comfortable with the retirement saving strategy that we are cobbling together," Jim started. "You've probably noticed by now that we actuaries like looking at the past. There is so much data to analyze, and whatever may have happened, we can always rationalize why. But when all is said and done, we can't live in the past."

Jim paused briefly after he said this.

"From this point on," he continued, "we are going to do something considerably more difficult; we will try to forecast the *next* 30 years. This brings to mind what Yogi Berra once said about forecasts: 'It is hard to make predictions, especially about the future.'

"I would note that it is more than just hard, it is literally impossible to make a prediction that you can totally rely on. I think it was John Kenneth Galbraith who said, 'There are two kinds of forecaster — those who don't know and those who don't know they don't know.' I like to think I'm the first type, but sometimes I have my doubts. All I'm saying is, take everything I say from here on in with a grain of salt, and do the same with anyone else who is brave or foolhardy enough to tell you what they think is going to happen."

"You mean like my barber," Brett quipped.

"Yes," Jim chuckled, "like your barber. Given the difficulty of forecasting, you might be wondering why you can't just settle for the analysis we've done up until now and cross our fingers that the future will be no worse. After all, I've told you that you should take some comfort in knowing that the saving strategy we have created would have weathered even the worst-ever 30-year historical period and would have done brilliantly in a typical 30-year period."

Brett interjected, "Actually, I do take some comfort in that. As far as I'm concerned, you've already done more for us than we could ever have hoped for. That first day, when I asked you how much we should be saving, you could have just told me 12 percent of pay and sent me on my way. But if the future is unknowable, as your friend Galbraith says, why bother trying to forecast it?"

"There is something in what you say," Jim admitted, "but I still feel I owe it to you to go that extra mile and try to peer into the future. For sure, it is not totally predictable, but nor is it a total mystery. To the extent that it is affected by the flapping of a butterfly's wings, we can't expect to guess what will happen. However, the future is also the result of major changes that are taking place in the world around us, and their impact is easier to predict. The signs of change could already be in the air and could be giving us a glimpse of what is to come. My hope is that we can interpret them correctly. If the next 30 years will be essentially the same as some past period, we now know we don't have to worry too much; I have already shown that you can survive it. If it turns out to be fundamentally different, however, we want as much advance warning as possible.

"Consider the analogy with climate change. It would be delusional to try to predict the weather on a specific day three weeks from now. On the other hand, predicting the climate 20 years from now seems much more plausible. We would need to be wilfully blind not to see the harbingers of a changing climate: rising sea temperatures, melting ice caps and so on. It is important to try to gauge where all of that is leading us. Ideally, we will guess right and be able to act on that information before it is too late."

"Are you saying the economy is like the climate, on the verge of a major change?" asked Megan.

"It seems very likely. Just as we've recently witnessed hotter summers than we have ever had before, we are also witnessing events in the capital markets that would have been unthinkable just 30 years ago, such as near-zero interest rates and stubbornly low inflation. They happen for a reason.

"Over the next few sessions, I want to explain how the capital markets are charting a new course. We'll try to use that information to make an educated guess of how they will shape key metrics, like inflation and interest rates. Having done that, we can then make a forecast of how they will affect saving for retirement."

"That sounds like an ambitious plan," said Megan.

"It is," agreed Jim. "And while we won't get everything right, I would put it to you that we're better off trying than not trying."

"I know actuaries make forecasts all the time," Megan observed. "Is there anything from your long experience that you can use to guide you?"

"The biggest forecasting pitfall is what actuaries describe as 'giving undue weight to the immediate past,'" Jim replied. "It is human nature to be too heavily influenced by what has happened recently and to dismiss the more distant past as irrelevant. It's not a big problem if we're only forecasting five years into the future, but it gets us into trouble in longer-term forecasts. For instance, when nominal interest rates were double digits in the 1980s, actuaries would have typically forecast that interest rates would remain around 7 to 10 percent for the long term. That obviously didn't happen."

"Good to know," said Megan. "How do you guard against giving 'undue weight'?"

"It's hard, but it helps to balance it by applying 'reversion to the mean,'" replied Jim. "When a given economic variable gets too far removed from its long-term average, we ask ourselves whether this is the new norm or just a short-term aberration. It's usually the latter and, usually, the variable in question that has gone so far off-track eventually returns closer to its long-term average.

"Once again, consider the challenge for actuaries around 1990. The inflation rate in the previous 20 years (1971 to 1990) had been very high. It had topped 10 percent in the worst years, and the annual average had been 7 percent. This level of inflation hadn't been seen in the previous two centuries or probably ever. Still, if you had asked an actuary at the time for their long-term forecast for inflation, the consensus would have been around 5 or 6 percent. The long-term average up to 1990, however, was closer to 3 percent. If we had taken that into account, we would have been more accurate in forecasting the eventual drop in inflation."

Brett and Megan stayed quiet, secretly hoping Jim was ready to move on.

Jim could sense he was being gently nudged along and asked, "Shall we get started then?"

"Yes!" they both responded.

Inflation

"I just mentioned inflation, which is as good a starting point as any. By 'inflation,' I mean the average annual increase in consumer prices as measured by the Consumer Price Index for Canada. Guessing future inflation is either really easy or really hard. It's easy if we believe there will always be some upward pressure on prices, as there has been ever since World War II. This graph shows the Canadian inflation rate since 1924."

"Inflation has been more or less under control in Canada since 1990. I believe that this is partly due to actions taken by the Bank of Canada."

"What can the Bank of Canada do about it?" asked Megan.

"They can adjust the overnight rate of interest to make it harder or easier to obtain loans. In this way, they can either apply a brake on the economy or step on the gas pedal. It was in 1991 that the Bank of Canada first set its target of 2 percent annual inflation. Together with the Government of Canada, it reviews this target every five years. Over the last 30 years, it has seen fit to maintain the target at 2 percent."

"Has the Bank of Canada been successful in keeping inflation close to the target?"

Figure 17: History of price inflation in Canada

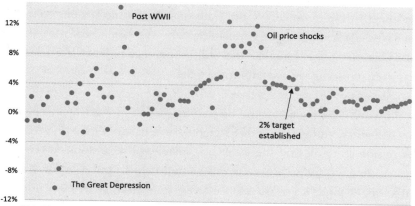

"Extremely successful, or maybe just lucky," replied Jim. "Since 1995, the average change in CPI has been 1.9 percent a year, and the yearly change has rarely deviated more than 1 percent from the Bank's target."

"Why do you say that guessing future inflation might be really hard, then?" asked Megan.

"Because it may not always be so easy to keep inflation in check. We don't know what sort of economic storms we will face along the way. Look at the reaction to the COVID-19 pandemic from both the Bank of Canada and the Government of Canada. The federal government's annual deficit ballooned more than tenfold in a matter of months, to over $300 billion. The Bank of Canada signalled it would be as accommodating as possible for as long as needed until we got over the economic effects of the pandemic. The trouble is that it is easy to overshoot and create higher inflation in the process. So far, that hasn't happened — at least as far as the price of goods and services are concerned — but it doesn't mean we're safe."

Megan followed up, "You're afraid, then, that we might be underestimating future inflation?"

"Well, yes. That, or we might go in the other direction and have to worry about *deflation* some day."

"You mean prices actually dropping?" interjected Brett.

"Correct. That might seem impossible, since inflation is all we've known since World War II, but we had deflation during the Great Depression, and prices were essentially flat in both the US and the UK between 1800 and World War II. An aging population makes it possible, and maybe even plausible, that something like this will happen again. Japan, for instance, has been wrestling with deflation since the 1990s."

"What's your best guess, then?" asked Brett.

"I would still say 2 percent, despite my deflation worries and despite my concern about giving undue weight to recent experience. First, I have no reason to think that the Bank of Canada will abandon the target it has maintained for 30 years, so this should help to put a lid on higher inflation. Second, it's in no one's interest to encourage or even tolerate deflation, which makes it less likely that it will happen. Finally, the current inflation rate is very close to the long-term mean as well as the shorter-term mean.

"Having said all that," Jim added, "I wouldn't be surprised to see it inch down to 1 percent."

Salary Increases

"Next, we'll talk about wage inflation. In general, wages and salaries tend to rise faster than price inflation, and that's without taking promotions into account. The gap between wage and price inflation isn't as big as it used to be, though." Jim handed out a chart to show them what he was talking about.

"During most of the 1940s, 1950s and 1960s, the average national wage in Canada was rising faster than price inflation by roughly 2 percent a year. Indeed, over some 10-year periods, like 1952 to 1961, wage increases outstripped price inflation by more than 3 percent a year. By the 1970s, though, this period of robust wage increases came to a screeching halt."

"Why?" asked Megan.

"There are several possible explanations. A lot of nation-building was going on after the war, which meant workers were in short supply from the 1940s until the mid-1960s and companies were willing to pay more to keep them. In addition, the private sector unions were powerful then, and

Figure 18: Wages tend to rise faster than prices

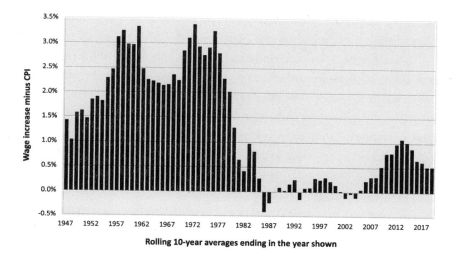

strikes for higher wages were common. In the 1960s, Canada had one of the highest rates in the world for days lost due to strikes. It was easier for unions to be more demanding in those days, since globalization hadn't yet emerged on a large scale. Factories and jobs weren't being moved abroad yet to less expensive locales.

"Then the 1970s came and the baby boomers hit the job market like a tsunami. Unemployment rose and, by the law of supply and demand, it reduced pressure on employers to increase wages. Everyone in the Western world also felt poorer after the oil price shocks. For the period 1973 to 1982, for instance, wage increases exceeded price inflation by only 0.4 percent a year on average. In the 1980s and 1990s, these pressures were still being felt and were exacerbated by the impact of globalization. Manufacturing plants moved offshore and took jobs with them. Workers elsewhere were willing to work for much less money, so in a way, they were exporting wage deflation to North America and Europe."

"How do you mean?" asked Megan.

"When the same work can be done more cheaply in another part of the world, it has a dampening effect on places where wages are still high," Jim explained. "Wage deflation isn't really exported, but international competition has the same effect. It's no surprise, then, that during this time, the differential between wage increases and price inflation in Canada practically disappeared."

"I see the chart shows a little bump upwards in wage inflation for 10-year periods ending after 2010," Brett noted.

"That's right," Jim said, nodding. "Unemployment in the past decade has fallen back to levels not seen since the 1960s, partly because baby boomers are leaving the workforce in large numbers. This has made workers more valuable than they have been for a long time. There may also have been some productivity increases thanks to technology. Even so, the differential between wage increases and price inflation is smaller than it used to be."

"Where do we go from here?" asked Megan.

"We do our best to extrapolate. I would base the extrapolation on the following storyline: Most of the baby boomers will be out of the job market within a few years. This will keep unemployment low and should create a little upward pressure on wages. Productivity should keep on improving as we get better at using technology and as more jobs are done remotely. Working from home was already a growing phenomenon before 2020, but it became a lot more widespread during the pandemic. This factor is also positive for wage growth. Globalization will not reverse anytime soon, but its effect on wages appears to be diminishing. After all, wages are catching up in the countries that took jobs from North America as a result of offshoring; they're not exporting their deflation to us as fast as they used to.

"On the negative side, the income gap between the haves and the have-nots has been growing in recent years as the owners of businesses seem to be keeping most of the profits to themselves rather than increasing wages. Another potentially negative factor is the rise of artificial intelligence (AI), which might be able to take over even skilled jobs and make labour less valuable."

"And the bottom line?"

"One can't be precise with so many moving pieces," Jim hedged, "but overall, my forecast is for moderate wage growth. Since we need a number to feed into our spreadsheet, I suggest we assume that wages will grow faster than prices by 1 percent a year. This growth rate is not as high as it was in the '50s and '60s, but it is higher than in the '80s and '90s."

"You're saying we can expect our pay levels to rise by only 1 percent a year?" asked Megan.

"Oh no, that's just the differential between price inflation and general wage inflation," Jim replied. "If you can visualize it, your pay increases are made up of three parts. The first part represents price inflation. You'd expect wages to at least keep up with prices, otherwise you'd have a revolution on your hands. The second part is the excess of general wage inflation over price inflation, which is the part I'm predicting will be 1 percent a year. The third part reflects whatever extra pay increases you get for promotions or simply getting better at your own job. Some people call the third part 'merit pay.'"

Brett observed, "I guess merit pay can be all over the map."

"Yes, it can," Jim confirmed. "The higher your education level, the more chance you'll see bigger merit pay increases over your career. Typically, the bigger increases tend to be concentrated in the first 10 to 15 years of one's career. For this exercise, I need to come up with a reasonable scale of salary increases, so I propose to use the following." Jim showed them a table he had labelled Table 10.

Table 10: Future pay increases for Brett and Megan

	Merit pay	General wage inflation	Price inflation	Total pay increase
Years 1 to 10	4%	1%	2%	7%
Years 11 to 20	2%	1%	2%	5%
Years 21 to 25	0%	1%	2%	3%
Years 26 to 30	−1%	1%	2%	2%

Megan seemed dubious. "It's hard to believe that my pay is going to go up by 7 percent a year for the next 10 years."

"You're quite right in thinking that isn't how it's going to happen," Jim acknowledged. "More likely, you'll see pay increases in the 3- to 4-percent range for most years but then get a bump of 10 percent or more when you receive a promotion. Rather than trying to guess exactly when those promotions will happen, I've used a smoothed scale that has the same general effect."

"How does your forecast for overall pay increases compare with historical increases?" asked Brett.

"If you're looking at just nominal amounts (that is, the total increase in pay), future pay increases should be lower, since we're forecasting inflation to be lower. If you mean real pay increases (over and above inflation), I'm expecting they will be lower than they were before 1970 but higher than they have been ever since then. Merit increases depend on the individual, and I have no good reason to think they will be different in the future."

Brett thought about that for a moment. "Do smaller pay increases make it harder to save for retirement?"

Jim replied, "Just the opposite! If your goal is to produce retirement income equal to a certain percentage of your final average salaries, that number won't be as high relative to your earnings earlier in your career as it would be if wage increases were higher."

"Not sure I follow, Jim. Could you try again?"

"Essentially, your retirement income goal is a certain percentage of your final employment income; call it 50 percent. All things being equal, it's easier to reach 50 percent of a smaller number than 50 percent of a bigger number.

"Consider my prediction of pay increases to be a small positive in your overall forecast. I wouldn't worry about it too much, one way or the other. Rather, future interest rates and stock market returns will really dictate how much you'll have to save. We'll talk about that next time. For now, we'll complete lines one and two of our forecast."

Here is what Jim wrote on the whiteboard:

Table 11: Best estimate of future inflation

Price inflation (annual change in CPI)	2%
Wage inflation in excess of price inflation	1%

Brett wasn't quite done yet. "Final question, Jim. How do your numbers jibe with forecasts from other sources?"

"As it turns out, my forecasts for both price inflation and general wage inflation are precisely the same as were used by the Chief Actuary for the

Canada Pension Plan in the last actuarial valuation of that plan. This is a coincidence, since I didn't check that valuation until after I made my own forecast."

"Does that similarity increase your confidence in your forecast?"

"Not one iota," said Jim, smiling.

At this point, Brett stretched his arms wide, which had become the unofficial signal that he had reached the limit of his attention span.

Jim suggested they adjourn for the day and take up the discussion the following Saturday.

CHAPTER 16

Bonds Will Underperform

Saturday, August 20

The next time they met, Jim started with a preamble. "Last time we met, we covered both price and wage inflation. Now we'll turn our sights on interest rates. The direction of interest rates is important if bonds are going to form a part of your asset mix, and it may even be important if you don't invest in bonds. For a given level of risk, you want to get the highest possible return; and when interest rates are very low, as they are now, achieving the desired return becomes more of a challenge.

"When I talk about bonds, I mean government bonds like the long-Canada bonds we have talked about in past sessions. These bonds pay out interest regularly, usually in the form of semi-annual coupons. At the end of the term, the initial amount invested is paid back to you at par. If you buy a $1,000 bond at par with a nominal 3 percent yield, paid semi-annually, the effective annual yield will be slightly more than 3 percent — actually, 3.022 percent in this case — because of the timing of the payments."

"That's not much of a payout," Megan observed. "Is that what bonds are offering these days?"

"Well, as a matter of fact, yields are even lower than that. Nominal yields on longer-term bonds are between 1 and 2 percent."

Megan made a face. "That's terrible!"

"It is if most of your saving days are ahead of you," Jim responded. "Having said that, in spite of the super-low yields that bonds offer these days, the annual return on bonds has been pretty good for a long time; even spectacular, in some years."

"How is that possible when yields are so low?" asked Brett.

"It's possible because yields weren't always that low," Jim explained. "The interest that a bond pays out makes up only a part of the return on that bond. The other part is a capital gain or capital loss as the market value of the bond changes. We will get to that in due course. First though, let's take a closer look at bond yields.

"Anyone under 60 has seen interest rates in general, and bond yields in particular, moving in just one direction their whole adult lives — down. In 1980, the yields on long-term Government of Canada bonds hit 15.2 percent. The yields on provincial and corporate bonds, as well as the interest rates on mortgages, would have been even higher than that. It got that high for a number of reasons, but mainly because inflation was a big problem at the time. High interest rates tend to reduce inflation, since they make it hard to borrow and that puts the brakes on the economy."

Jim handed out a chart to show these trends.

"Then yields started dropping. Apart from a little uptick in the late 1980s, the yield on long-term bonds has fallen more or less in a straight line.

"The funny thing about bonds," Jim continued, "is that when yields go down, bond *prices* go up. Just a minute ago, I gave you the example of a $1,000 bond with a 3 percent yield that was purchased at par. If investors generally demanded a greater return than 3 percent — say, 4 percent — the bond would have to sell for considerably less than $1,000. As a result, dropping yields lead to capital gains and rising yields lead to capital losses. This capital gain or capital loss makes up the other part of the return on bonds."

Megan was a little troubled by this. "I knew stocks were risky and I sort of knew that real estate was risky, but now you're telling me we can lose money even with bonds!"

Brett wondered aloud, "If we still wanted to invest in bonds, how would we go about it?"

Figure 19: Long-term bond yields are bottoming out

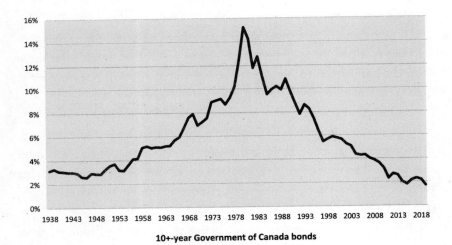

10+-year Government of Canada bonds

"You would buy into a bond mutual fund or a bond ETF, which is pretty much the same thing but with lower fees. These investments represent a pool of many bonds, and the return is made up of the interest the bonds pay plus any capital gain or loss."

Brett jumped in. "You were saying that bond returns have been pretty good, even though bond yields have been low. Just how good have they been?"

Jim corrected him, "To be more precise, bond returns have been good because yields have been going lower, not because they're low. It's the direction of yields that dictates capital gains or losses, not the absolute level. To answer your question, over the 40-year period from 1980 to 2019, the average annual return (compounded) on long-Canada bonds was 8.7 percent a year after fees. By comparison, the average inflation rate over the same period was just 3.0 percent. That means the real return was 5.5 percent.[1] Part of that return came from the high yields that bonds offered earlier in that period, and the other part came from capital gains as yields fell. You would have done well to have invested 40 percent of your investment portfolio in long-term bonds during that time."

---

1   1.087 / 1.03 = 1.055

Brett pondered this before speaking. "Judging from that type of performance, it sounds like long-term bonds might be a good place to be over the next 30 years."

Jim shook his head. "Unfortunately, that is extremely unlikely, if not impossible. The very reason for the great returns in the last 40 years is also the reason why bonds will probably do quite poorly over the next 30 or so years."

"You've lost me."

"Take another look at the chart," said Jim. "Bonds made great capital gains because yields fell from 15 percent in the early 1980s to the present level of 1 percent. To duplicate that feat, bond yields would have to fall by that much again, which would bring the yield down to negative 13 percent. Obviously, that's not going to happen.

"There are really just two plausible scenarios for future yields. In the first scenario, they might rise, thus 'reverting to the mean.' Don't expect to see 15 percent yields again, but they might get up to 5 percent. If yields do go up, you'll be getting higher interest payments on your bonds in future years, but you'll also be incurring capital losses. The one will more or less offset the other, so the net result could very well be a nominal return of close to zero. The real return might be negative."

"Frankly, that sounds rather far-fetched," Brett declared.

"No, it's quite possible," replied Jim. "Bonds have had prolonged periods of negative returns. Consider the period from 1951 to 1980, for example. Yields on long-term Canada bonds went from 3.7 percent to 15.2 percent over that 30-year stretch. You would have received a pretty good return based on those yields, but that would have been offset by capital losses as the yields rose. In fact, the average nominal return on long-term bonds over that period was just 2.4 percent a year. If you think that doesn't sound so bad compared to the low present-day yields, note that the average *real* return over that period was a negative 1.8 percent a year."

"You mean . . ." Megan started, and Jim completed her sentence.

"Yes, you would have been losing money in real terms throughout that period. It seems history is very likely to repeat itself in the years ahead. You see, bonds differ in one fundamental aspect from stocks. With stocks, you never know for sure how they will behave, since so many factors can affect the market. Interest rates are just one of them. By contrast, you can get a pretty good idea of the future return on bonds largely from the yield at the start of the period. With yields being so low these days, we can't expect much from long-term bonds for decades, even if yields start to rise."

"You mentioned a second scenario?" asked Megan.

"Yes, bond yields might stay low for a long time to come," replied Jim. "In this case, you won't be incurring large capital losses on bonds, but then again, your overall return will be pretty miserable given that the yields will be so low. As you can see from Figure 19, history can't tell us much about this scenario because we've never really had a prolonged period in which interest rates remained at a very low level. Maybe we did in the 1800s, but there wasn't much of a bond market then and there are no reliable records from that time. This is essentially a new phenomenon that some people refer to as 'low for long.' This situation is great for borrowers but not good at all for savers."

"What are the chances of a future with 'low-for-long' interest rates?" asked Megan.

"Unfortunately, the chances are very good. I'll explain why next time. Can we save that for next Saturday?"

CHAPTER 17

Interest Rates Will Remain "Low for Long"

Friday, August 26 and Saturday, August 27

It had been nearly three weeks since Jim had told Megan his daughter's name, and Megan had been thinking about Alyssa ever since. That Friday night over dinner she gave Brett a progress report on her investigation.

"I talked to Mrs. Gladstone again. Apparently, Alyssa works in the financial industry, but Mrs. Gladstone didn't know where. It was easy to find out, though. I googled her name and found out that she works as a financial planner for one of the big banks."

Brett frowned. "Do you really think you should be digging into Jim's personal life like this?"

"I'm sure he'd like to reconcile with his daughter. Wouldn't you?"

Brett knew it was best to leave Megan to her own devices. As if he had a choice.

The following day, they met at Jim's place as usual.

Jim started the discussion by saying, "It seems a little cruel to subject you to a discussion of bonds two sessions in a row, but it's best to get it over with. Sort of like eating your green beans before tackling the steak.

"I promised you I would explain why interest rates, including bond yields, will probably remain low for a very long time to come. You could be forgiven for thinking that rates are so low right now because of two significant and fairly recent events, but the real reason is something else entirely."

Brett and Megan visibly perked up. It was so unlike Jim to inject a little drama into his explanations.

"The first event I'm referring to is the global financial meltdown of 2008–09, what some people call the 'Great Recession.' When it happened, governments scrambled to bring interest rates down quickly to get the world economies back on their feet. Most notably, the US created liquidity by buying up government debt, a program they called 'quantitative easing.' In fact, they ran this program twice, once in 2008–09 and again in 2010. These two programs were coined 'QE1' and 'QE2.' There was also a QE3 in 2013, but that was less successful and we can ignore it for our purposes.

"QE1 and QE2 were huge buying programs designed to inject new money into the economy. In QE1, which started in November 2008, the US Federal Reserve bought up $600 billion worth of government bonds. That artificial demand drove up the price of the bonds and thus drove down the yields. (Remember, bond prices and bond yields move in opposite directions.) By 2010, the Fed determined that the economy wasn't growing quickly enough, so it launched into a second round of buying. Another $600 billion in bonds were purchased by the second quarter of 2011."

"And you're saying QE1 and QE2 didn't bring down interest rates much?" asked Brett.

"They certainly brought them down a little and they helped to bring both the stock markets and the economy back to life, but as you saw in Figure 19, interest rates had already been coming down well before QE. These massive bond-buying programs just accelerated the process."

"You mentioned two events," said Megan. "What was the other one?"

"When the COVID-19 pandemic was declared in March of 2020, global economies practically ground to a halt. Unemployment hit levels not seen since the Great Depression, and stock markets plunged at a record pace. Governments knew they had to do something to keep the economies going and so, once again, a massive amount of money was injected into economies in all high-income countries. Both the Bank of Canada and the

US Federal Reserve vowed to keep interest rates as low as possible for as long as necessary.

"This massive intervention in the capital markets had an effect, of course. The nominal yield on Government of Canada 10-year bonds dropped in early 2020 to about one-half of 1 percent. But note that the yield in February 2020, the month before the pandemic was declared, was just 1.2 percent, so yields were already low. That 1.2 percent yield happened a good 10 years after the Great Recession was over and before the COVID-19 pandemic started. Bond yields wouldn't be that low because of an event that happened 10 years before, nor could they have been so low because of a pandemic that hadn't happened yet. What was the cause?"

Brett and Megan knew a rhetorical question when they heard one, so they simply nodded and waited for Jim to continue.

"The real reason for the persistently low interest rates we've experienced, and also the reason they will stay low for a long time to come, is demographics."

"Say what?" asked Brett.

"Demographics. Specifically, the age distribution of the population. To be even more specific, the proportion of the population that is over 55 is growing."

"Why should that affect interest rates?" asked Megan.

"It's all about supply and demand," Jim replied. "Imagine if everybody wanted to borrow money and few people were willing to lend it. What do you think that would do to interest rates?"

Once again, this sounded rhetorical, but this time Jim appeared to be waiting for an answer.

"I guess it would raise them," ventured Megan. "The few lenders would figure they could hold out for a higher interest rate, since not all borrowers could afford to walk away. The lender would just find someone else who wanted to borrow and who would pay higher interest."

"Exactly!" said Jim, smiling. "Supply and demand. Now let's say you have two people, one age 60 and the other age 35. Who is more likely to lease a car, start a business that requires capital or need a mortgage to buy a house?"

Brett decided to get in on the action. "It would be the younger guy."

"I'd didn't say they were both guys," Jim noted, "but yes, you're basically right. No doubt you can see where I'm going with this. If you had to guess who had a paid-off car and a paid-off home and also had some savings tucked away, that would be . . ."

"The older guy — um, person— of course," Brett responded. "But not every older person has money and not every younger person is looking to borrow."

"Not everyone, true enough," agreed Jim. "But it is *broadly* true that older people are the ones with money and younger people are the ones who need it. I know no one likes labels, but it will make it easier to get my next point across. So, let's refer to people age 55 to 80 as Savers and those age 25 to 54 as Borrowers. In the 1990s and earlier, money was scarce because the Savers were greatly outnumbered. In 1993, for instance, there were only 39 Savers in Canada for every 100 Borrowers. It's no accident that risk-free government bonds were paying a real yield of over 4 percent.

"Then the baby boomers started to turn grey and the ratio of Savers to Borrowers started to rise rather quickly. By 2003, there were 44 Savers for every 100 Borrowers and by 2013, it had jumped to 57. Today, there are more than 70 Savers for every 100 Borrowers."

"Wow!" exclaimed Megan. "The Canadian population seems to be aging fast. Will this trend continue?"

"Actually," said Jim, "the saver to borrower ratio will rise a tiny bit more and then stabilize. It will do so, however, at the highest level it has ever been. Moreover, it won't be going down for several decades at least. Even high immigration rates won't change that.

"As the number of savers grew after 2000, my supply-demand argument suggests we should have seen interest rates falling, and that is precisely what happened. Note that this trend started before the 2007 US housing crisis and certainly before the 2008–09 financial meltdown. It started when the ratio of savers to borrowers started to rise."

"How can you be sure it's not a coincidence that rates fell when the population started to age?" asked Megan. "How do you know the real cause wasn't something else?"

"That's a fair question, Megan," Jim conceded. "But what would that something else be? Whatever it was, it would have to affect highly developed economies everywhere, since this phenomenon of falling rates is widespread. An alternative explanation, I suppose, is that all governments had suddenly become more responsible and started to rein in their deficits. I suppose this might have caused interest rates to fall. But that is not what governments were doing. Perhaps consumers in all developed countries suddenly started to spend less and save more. But that didn't happen either."

Jim continued to expound his theory. "Here is another piece of evidence to back the notion that demographics are causing interest rates to fall. Another country went through the aging process years before Canada: Japan. That country's population started to age nearly two decades earlier than Canada's. As Table 12 shows, Japan's ratio of savers to borrowers in 1975 was remarkably similar to Canada's ratio 18 years later, in 1993. Similarly, Japan in 1985 looked like Canada in 2003, and the same is true for the next two decades as well."

Table 12: Ratio of savers (55–80) to borrowers (25–54)

	Japan	Canada (18 years later)
1975	33%	39%
1985	43%	44%
1995	56%	57%
2005	74%	73%*

*Estimated ratio in 2023 based on a medium-growth scenario

"Table 13 shows how 10-year government bond yields in each country changed over the same period," said Jim. "As you can see, Canada has been tracking interest rates in Japan with almost uncanny precision."

Table 13: 10-year government bond yield

	Japan	Canada (18 years later)
1975	8.2%	8.0%
1985	6.6%	4.5%
1995	2.9%	2.3%
2005	1.4%	1.4%*

*Yield in early 2021, 16 years later

"The trend toward even lower rates in Japan continued after 2005. Currently, its 10-year bond yield is very close to 0 percent and it has flirted with negative rates, which is a concept that even actuaries have trouble getting their minds around."

"What does all this mean for Canada?" asked Megan.

"In 2019, I wrote an article in which I predicted that nominal yields on Canada 10-year bonds would drop very close to 0 percent by 2037. At the time, this forecast seemed a little far-fetched, but that is what the yields in Japan were suggesting. Then the pandemic hit and Canada bond yields fell to 50 basis points, which put us many years ahead of schedule. Yields falling to 0 percent are more plausible than I thought."

"I have to admit, the similarities between Japan and Canada are pretty remarkable," Brett noted. "But maybe it's just a coincidence?"

"What if I told you that the same phenomenon is happening in other high-income countries? In particular, interest rates fell sooner and faster in Europe than they did in Canada. And guess what? The populations of the larger European nations are a little older than Canada's, which means they're following the same schedule relative to their aging process. In each country where the ratio of savers to borrowers reaches a certain threshold, interest rates and inflation start falling almost immediately."

"Aren't interest rates a little higher in the US than in Canada?" Brett queried.

"Yes, and the US has a slightly younger population than Canada, so once again, the trend is following the same pattern."

"Interesting," said Brett, "but what about China? They have a massive population and export their goods everywhere. Isn't it possible that the China influence will swamp what is happening elsewhere?"

"It would," Jim conceded, "if China still had a dynamic, young population. But surprisingly, China is aging quickly, too. You know that critical threshold for the ratio of savers to borrowers? China just crossed over it."

Brett threw his arms up in mock surrender. "Okay, I'm sold! Did you come up with this theory by yourself, Jim?"

"Actually, no. It first surfaced in a paper by Michael Walker that was published several years ago by the Fraser Institute. I simply built on it by taking a few years' more data and noting that the trend continues to hold."

As usual, it was Megan who brought the conversation back to Earth: "If we accept what you're saying, Jim, how does it affect your forecast for interest rates?"

Jim mulled that over for a moment before replying, "If I wanted to be dramatic, I would say that the aging population will result in several decades of near-zero inflation and near-zero interest rates in Canada. But let's back off that just a little. My guess is that bond yields will rise a little after the economic effects of COVID-19 have finally worn off. Because, at the end of the day, we're not quite Japan, are we? Besides, it's hard to believe there will be no reversion to the mean.

"In conclusion, I'm calling for the nominal yield on long-term bonds to settle at about 1.75 percent a year, which translates into a negative real yield of 0.25 percent."

"Wow! So, what's the point in investing in bonds at all?" asked Megan.

"That's a good question," Jim offered. "I would note that I've already had you reduce your bond position using a TDF approach. We'll still keep some bonds in your portfolio as you get older because (a) we could be wrong and (b) stocks might do even worse."

Brett looked troubled. "Jim, you've just finished explaining the difference between yields and returns. If the real yield is going to be negative, what is the return going to be?"

"Remember the other day when I mentioned to you that the real return on long bonds during the period 1951 to 1980 was negative 1.8 percent a year? I think we'll see a repeat of that phenomenon, though not quite as extreme. The portion of future returns due to yields will be lower than it was in the 1951–80 period, but the portion due to capital losses will also be lower. The net result, and this is just an educated guess, is an average real return on long-term Government of Canada bonds of negative 0.25 percent over the next 30 years."

Megan commented, "I'm starting to wish I'd been born in a different era."

"What, and miss out on smartphones? At least you're benefitting from low interest rates on your mortgage," Jim noted. "We'll continue completing our table of assumptions," he said as he added another line to the forecast on the whiteboard. "Here is where we stand."

Table 14: Jim's updated forecast

Price inflation (CPI)	2.0%
Wage inflation in excess of price inflation	1.0%
Average return on long-term bonds (real)	−0.25%

"What are we going to tackle next?" asked Brett as he started to stretch.

"Stocks," said Jim. "You'll need to be fresh for that, so we will save it for another day. Will you be around for the long weekend?"

CHAPTER 18

The Unpredictable Stock Market

Saturday, September 3

The next session fell on the Labour Day long weekend, but no one had plans, so they kept to the usual Saturday time slot. Jim thought it best to start with a warning.

"In the last three sessions, we covered inflation and bond yields. I'm not saying that those variables are easy to predict, but one can at least weave a compelling story about the direction in which each of them is headed. Today, we are going to venture into the most difficult part of our economic forecast: stocks. If inflation and interest rates are like two old mares in our stable, then stocks would be the untamed stallion."

"Very nice metaphor, Jim!" Megan said appreciatively.

Jim smiled back and continued. "What we are going to do today is forecast future stock returns by approaching the problem from three perspectives. The first is by looking at real returns over different past periods.

Real Returns

"You'll recall that the average real return on stocks has exceeded 6 percent over very long periods, going back, in fact, to 1924 in Canada and 1801 in the US. Your investment horizon, however, is a lot shorter than that. It is closer to 40 years, if you include some of the years after retirement when you still have significant assets. If we measure real returns on stocks over 40-year periods, we find they have been quite volatile. Between 1925 and 1964, for instance, the average real return was 8.8 percent. This turned out to be the highest ever over a 40-year stretch, which I found quite remarkable given all the turmoil at the time. That period included both the Great Depression and World War II.

"The lowest average real return over a 40-year period was 4.1 percent, which occurred between 1969 and 2008. Ironically, there were no depressions or major wars during that time, but it did include the oil price shocks of the 1970s and a decade of 'stagflation.' It also included the dot-com bubble as well as the brunt of the 2008–09 global financial meltdown.

"Based on history alone, we might therefore expect the real return over the next 30 to 40 years to land somewhere between 4 and 8 percent. If we want to justify an estimate outside this range, there has to be something about the future that will be fundamentally different from anything in our past. What would that be?"

Brett and Megan looked at Jim expectantly.

"Oh, I was hoping you would tell me," Jim clarified. "As a hint, consider our bond discussion the other day."

Brett and Megan were silent for a minute, deep in thought.

Then Megan blurted out, "Demographics! That's what's different!"

Jim's eyes lit up with delight. "Very good, Megan! Can you expand on that?"

"From what you told us previously, we're getting older as a population, which means fewer borrowers and more savers. That is why interest rates are so low and why they're going to stay low." Suddenly, Megan looked a little troubled. "But I don't understand what that has to do with stock market returns. I thought the demographic argument explained why interest rates and bond yields would stay low. Why would it affect the stock market?"

"Remember," said Jim, "stocks compete with bonds for investor money. If bond yields go down, investors should be bidding up the price of stocks, since they would offer a more attractive return. As the price of stocks goes higher, however, their potential for future growth will diminish. Stocks will eventually reach the point where their prospective return is no greater than is needed to maintain their attractiveness versus bonds."

Megan grew even more confused. "If falling bond yields mean stock prices go up even faster, then why are you suggesting that future stock market returns will be lower than they have been historically?"

"It's because those bond yields are no longer falling. They have pretty much hit rock bottom. The time is fast approaching when the upward adjustment to stock prices should also hit a ceiling. This isn't to say that stocks can't keep rising beyond that point; they'll just rise more slowly than what we've seen in recent years. What I think we are witnessing is a once-in-a-generation repricing of stocks to reflect an era of unprecedented low inflation and low interest rates. Future increases in stock prices will be harder to come by, and that means lower returns."

Brett offered, "If real returns have been in the 4 to 8 percent range, you're saying they'll be closer to 4 percent rather than 8 percent in the future."

"Or perhaps lower than 4 percent, depending on whether interest rates start to move up," Jim replied.

P/E Ratios

"Another way to tackle the question is to examine trends in the price-to-earnings ratios on stocks."

"What is that ratio, exactly?" asked Brett.

"In the case of an individual stock, the price-to-earnings ratio is the price of the stock divided by its annual earnings. Let's call it 'P/E ratio' for short. For instance, a stock priced at $100 with annual earnings of $5 per share has a P/E ratio of 20. The higher the P/E ratio, the higher the value placed on the stock. The same thinking applies to the stock market index as a whole. The P/E ratio for the S&P 500 index (which you'll recall is the main index for US stocks) normally fluctuates between 10 and 20. When the P/E ratio gets too high, it can be a sign that stocks are overvalued and that a correction is in store. The P/E ratio over the last 120 years has been 16.2 on average. Compare that to the current P/E ratio, which is over 35. Take a look at this chart."

Figure 20: Price-to-earnings ratios (S&P 500)

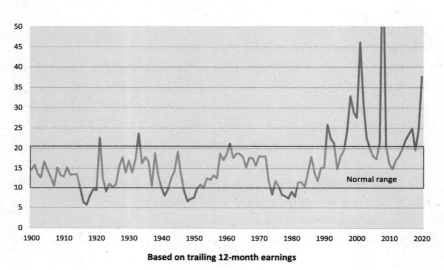

Based on trailing 12-month earnings

Brett whistled. "I guess that means stocks are way overvalued?"

"You would think so," Jim replied, "but it's not as clear-cut as that. It is true that the P/E ratio has been as high as 35 only twice before, and both times it meant trouble. It happened in 2001 around the time of the dot-com bubble and in 2008 during the global financial meltdown. Based on those precedents, the current situation does give the impression of being overvalued.

"On the other hand, interest rates have never been this low before. As I was just explaining, stocks are affected by interest rates almost as much as bonds are, though the relationship isn't quite as direct in the case of stocks. In theory, the stock price should be the present value of future dividends. For a given stream of future dividends on a stock, lower interest rates should translate into a higher stock price. Interest rates are currently low enough to justify a P/E ratio of 35 or even higher, assuming dividend growth remains untouched.

"On the other hand, whatever is causing the low interest rates (and I think it's demographics) may also cause company earnings to grow more slowly in the future. As a result, the dividends on those stocks might grow more slowly, too. If so, stocks may be overvalued after all."

Jim paused when he saw the slightly glazed look on the faces of his captive audience. Brett, in particular, really looked like he wanted to stretch but knew it wasn't time yet.

Jim decided to cut back on the theorizing. "There is really no point in trying to dig deeper into this question, because no matter how much we try to get to the bottom of it, the stock market has a propensity to surprise us. Here is what I think sounds most plausible given the facts:

- P/E ratios will contract somewhat from their current high levels,
- interest rates will probably rise a little rather than a lot over the next 30 years and
- real growth in the earnings of companies will be modestly dampened because of demographics.

"As a result," Jim concluded, "I believe that real returns on stocks in the future will be closer to the bottom end of their historical range."

Brett didn't look convinced. "I sort of get it, but then again, you told us a while ago that US stocks have been achieving real growth of over 6 percent for over two centuries. Do you have any tangible evidence to suggest that the party is over?"

Jim shrugged his shoulders. "Remember earlier I was telling you about how real returns on stocks of 6 to 7 percent over the long term seemed to be the norm in most developed countries? The one exception is Japan. The long-term real return on Japanese stocks since the 1920s has been closer to 3 percent rather than 6 percent. Furthermore, the Nikkei 225 is still 40 percent below its 1989 peak.

"That piece of data is not conclusive, but you could interpret it as indirect evidence of what happens to stocks when a population is aging and interest rates have bottomed out. Since the 1990s, Japanese interest rates have remained near zero and its stock market returns have trailed most other high-income countries."

"What is your conclusion from all this?" asked Megan.

"I'm inclined to go with a real return on equities of 3.5 percent to 4 percent."

"That's pretty much the same conclusion as from your first way of looking at it," Megan observed. "Does that mean we have our answer?"

Jim shrugged and said, "If we wanted to get more actuarial, we could look at equity risk premiums and guess what direction they are going in."

"What's an equity risk premium?" Brett asked warily.

"It's the difference in return between stocks and low-risk investments like government bonds. Let's call it 'ERP' for short. The ERP tends to be a positive number because stocks should produce better returns than bonds over the longer term. After all, shareholders take more risk than bond-holders, and they expect to be compensated for it. If you measure it over the longest period for which I have Canadian data, which is 1924 to 2019, the ERP on Canadian equities versus long-term Canada bonds has been 3.3 percent a year, on average.

"If I went through the entire analysis, I could show you that the ERP tends to be higher over long periods when bond yields are rising, and lower when they're falling. We can dispense with all that, though, since the ulti-mate conclusion from analyzing ERPs is, once again, that real returns on stocks should be approximately 4 percent in the future."

This is the number that Jim wrote on the whiteboard.

Brett and Megan looked visibly relieved that they wouldn't be hearing anything more about equity risk premiums or about stock market fore-casts in general. The two were silent again as they considered what Jim had told them.

Megan finally asked, "How confident are you with your forecast?"

"Less confident than I was about inflation or bond returns, but that is the nature of the beast. One thing missing from this forecast is the impact of a black swan[1] event — like the Earth getting hit by an asteroid, an even

---

1   A term coined by Nassim Taleb in his book of that name.

bigger pandemic than we just had or AI changing our lives in ways that we can barely fathom."

"Does AI stand for 'actuarial intuition'?" asked Megan, tongue in cheek.

Jim answered that quip with a smile. "Getting the forecast right therefore involves more luck than skill. All I can say is, I've done the best I can with the data I have."

Brett looked deep in thought. "Even though you're saying stocks won't do nearly as well in the future as in the past, you're still suggesting we go ahead with the TDF approach, which involves investing 100 percent of our portfolio in stocks for the next few years."

Jim put down the whiteboard marker before responding. "We've already learned that the TDF approach would have worked better than a 60-40 mix over virtually any past 30-year period, even past periods when the real return on bonds was high. If we liked the TDF approach then, we should like it even more in an era when the real return on bonds may be negative.

"The only question is whether we should be even more aggressive in terms of our equity weighting than the TDF mix I had proposed to you.[2] Fortunately, that isn't a question you need to address for a long time to come, since you're going to be invested 100 percent in equities for a few years, anyway."

With that, Jim added the stock return forecast to the table on the whiteboard.

Table 15: Jim's whiteboard forecast

Inflation (annual change in CPI)	2.0%
Increase in average wages versus CPI	1.0%
Real return on long-term bonds	−0.25%
Real return on stocks	4.0%

"Is that it?" asked Megan hopefully. "Are we done with our long-term forecasting?"

"Well, we're done for today, if that helps," said Jim. "Next time we meet, we are going to conduct a reality check, and if it pans out, we'll apply these assumptions. That'll be the fun part."

---

2   Jim is talking about Table 8.

Brett and Megan weren't as confident about Jim's definition of "fun" as they were in his actuarial skills. Nevertheless, they confirmed that they would meet again the next Saturday and then walked home. Both of them felt an urgent need for some comfort food.

CHAPTER 19

Putting It All Together

Saturday, September 10

It wasn't until they were about to leave to go to Jim's place the next Saturday that Megan decided to give Brett an update on her activities. "I found which bank branch Alyssa works at and called her up," she informed him.

"Who?" asked Brett.

"Alyssa, Jim's daughter."

"Oh yeah, I'd hoped you had dropped this," he said.

"Not a chance. Anyway, I posed as a potential customer and arranged a meeting with her this coming Tuesday."

"You can't be serious!" exclaimed Brett.

"I'm totally serious. Jim has done a lot for us. This is the least we can do for him."

Brett didn't see it that way but knew it was best to let it go.

Jim greeted them at the door when they arrived and, after the usual pleasantries, led them to the living room, where the whiteboard was propped up on the mantel as usual. It still had the original forecast on it.

"Are we going to do some more work on the forecast?" asked Megan with some trepidation.

"Yes, but I'm not using the whiteboard immediately," Jim replied. "I needed to add a few columns, so I copied the information onto a spreadsheet and printed it out." He then handed out a sheet with an expanded table.

Table 16: Forecast versus long term

	Forecast next 30 years	The long term (1924–2019)	Difference
Inflation	2.0%	2.8%	−0.8%
Wage increases	1.0%	1.3%	−0.3%
Real return on bonds	−0.25%	3.1%	−3.35%
Real return on stocks	4.0%	6.6%	−2.6%

After staring at the new table for a few seconds, Megan said, "Very nice, Jim, but what is this for?"

"In the interests of producing a solid forecast, I want to be sure that our assumptions seem reasonable from all perspectives," Jim replied. "Looking at Table 16, does anything stand out?"

Megan was the first to volunteer a comment. "To me, two things stick out like a sore thumb. The negative real return on bonds and the low real return on stocks both stand out as unusual compared to how they have done over the long term."

"Right," said Jim. "You'll recall the rationale I previously provided for why our forecast assumptions are so much lower. Are you satisfied with that, or should we re-open the discussion?"

Brett answered quickly, "No, no, that's fine. I think we've covered them sufficiently."

"Excellent!" said Jim. "Next, we'll compare 'Forecast' to 'Last low-interest period.'"

With that, Jim handed out Table 17.

Table 17: Forecast versus a similar past period

	Forecast next 30 years	Last low-interest period (1934–67)	Difference
Inflation	2.0%	2.8%	−0.8%
Wage increases	1.0%	2.1%	−1.1%
Real return on bonds	−0.25%	0.2%	−0.45%
Real return on stocks	4.0%	8.2%	−4.2%

"Why are we making this comparison?" asked Brett.

"This is the last prolonged period when inflation and interest rates bore some resemblance to the current situation," Jim replied. "Do you see any anomalies?"

"Well, the real return on stocks looks awfully low," Megan replied.

"It does," Jim agreed. "But is it too low? I would note that the 'Last low-interest period' starts in 1934, in the midst of the Great Depression. This was after a record fall in the stock markets. Much of the reason for the high real return on stocks in that period is a rebound from extremely low levels. Would you say the same conditions exist today?"

Brett answered, "Not at all. You've made it clear that our starting point for stocks looks more like an extreme high than an extreme low. I'm convinced that we can't expect such high returns in the future."

"I'm glad you agree," said Jim. "It sounds like we can move on, then. Finally, we will compare 'Forecast' to the most recent period. The main reason for doing this is to ensure I didn't give 'undue weight' to the recent past, a common forecasting pitfall."

Jim handed out a third and final page, this one with a table labelled Table 18.

Table 18: Forecast versus the most recent 30 years

	Forecast next 30 years	Most recent 30 years (1990–2019)	Difference
Inflation	2.0%	2.0%	0%
Wage increases	1.0%	0.4%	0.6%
Real return on bonds	−0.75%	5.6%	−6.35%
Real return on stocks	3.75%	6.0%	−2.25%

Brett and Megan studied this table for a few seconds before Brett spoke, "I would say you definitely didn't give 'undue weight' to the last 30 years. Apart from the inflation rate, the forecast looks hugely different."

"Do you think we can justify the big differences?" Jim asked.

"Sure," said Brett. "Interest rates were coming down in the past 30 years, but that won't be happening in the next 30 years, so we know bond returns will have to drop a lot."

Megan was suddenly curious. "Jim, you've been asking what we think. What about you? Any second thoughts on your forecast?"

"I still stand by our forecast," Jim said. "But now that you ask the question, I have to admit to being a little uneasy about three of the assumptions. If I had to produce an alternate forecast, it would look like this." Jim then picked up his marker and added another column to the table on the whiteboard.

Table 19: An alternate forecast

	Main forecast	Alternate forecast
Inflation	2.0%	1.0%
Wage increases	1.0%	0.5%
Real return on bonds	−0.25%	0.25%
Real return on stocks	4.0%	5.0%

Jim explained, "I can easily see lower inflation, just like they had in Japan. Bonds might avoid a negative return and stocks might still find a way to produce a real return closer to the 100-year average."

"How much confidence do you have in your alternate forecast?" asked Brett.

"Put it this way," Jim replied, "if there were only two possible future scenarios, I'd give the main forecast a 75 percent probability and this alternate forecast 25 percent. That said, I think we are ready to run a projection using the main forecast assumptions. Would you both agree?"

Nods.

"Good, here comes the fun part. We will take the forecast assumptions and plug them into my spreadsheet. It's time to see whether the Rule of 30 still holds up under our forecast."

Jim now had the full attention of Brett and Megan.

He continued, "Just to remind you, the Rule of 30 involves saving 30 percent a year for retirement, less what you are spending in that year on:

a) mortgage payments or rent and
b) extraordinary, short-term, necessary expenses, like daycare.

"Also, it really only applies up until age 55 or so. Once you get that close to retirement, it makes more sense to save based on what a good retirement calculator tells you is appropriate given your actual situation at that time."

"Gotcha," Brett responded. He was anxious to see the results.

"We've seen that the Rule of 30 worked fairly well in worst-case historical scenarios such as 1946 to 1975. We have also seen that it produces even better results in more typical historical periods, like 1938 to 1967.

"On a philosophical note, I should add that I use the word 'typical' a little loosely in this context. In reality, there has been no such thing as a typical 30-year period in the past century. Every period is marked by one or more phenomena that you either assume or pray will never happen again: the Great Depression, World War II, the oil crisis, 9/11, the 2008–09 global financial meltdown and, most recently, the COVID-19 pandemic. You can't find a 30-year period that doesn't contain at least one black swan event of this magnitude. Since they are unpredictable by definition, I haven't tried to build one into our forecast, at least not explicitly. But perhaps one is implicitly built into the forecast given the way we created it."

Brett started to shift uncomfortably in his chair.

Jim saw what was happening and instantly picked up the pace. "In any event," he continued as he pointed to the whiteboard, "let's go straight to the results for our main forecast."

"I'm afraid to look," said Megan.

"Not to worry," Jim assured her. "Here it is."

Figure 21: The future based on Jim's main forecast

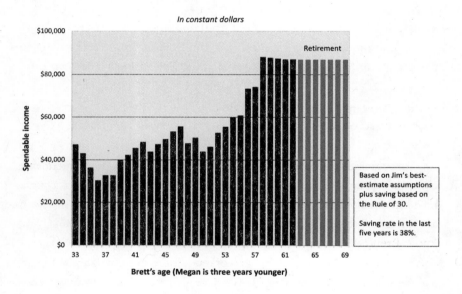

Megan was the first to react. "This is pretty close to what we're after, isn't it?"

"I think so," Jim concurred. "It would be even better if your spendable income didn't have those dips in your late 40s and early 50s, but that can't be helped if you keep on buying more expensive houses. Apart from that, your spendable income is generally rising throughout your careers and peaks in the final few working years. You can see that the same high level of spendable income is then maintained in real terms after you retire."

Brett was suspicious. "I thought our forecast for stock and bond returns was pretty miserable. How did we arrive at such a good result?"

"It's because I made use of our final enhancement," said Jim.

"You mean the one where you break away from the Rule of 30 near retirement?" Brett asked.

"Yes. In this case, the chart assumes you save based on the Rule of 30 until age 57, at which time you check on your progress with a retirement calculator. By doing that, you foresee a big rise in spendable income over your last five working years because you've eliminated the mortgage. While you'd love to spend all of it, the calculator shows you that that level of spending won't be sustainable for life. You therefore take advantage of the extra spendable income to increase your saving rate, which would lower your spendable income in those last five working years and raise it after retirement so the two balance out. The result is Figure 21."

Brett took a closer look at the chart. "By how much did you increase our saving rate in those last five working years?"

"By 8 percent," Jim replied, "which means you're saving 38 percent of pay at that point."

Brett was shocked. "We'd have to save 38 percent! How can we afford it?"

Jim remained patient, explaining, "Remember, it's all about spendable income. Saving 38 percent leaves you with a consistent amount of spendable income both before and after retirement."

Jim interpreted Brett's silence as skepticism, so he tried again. "You know, Brett, we've been through this. It is easier for you to save 38 percent of pay at age 60 than it is to save 8 percent at age 35. Look again at Figure 21. See how high your spendable income is during those last few working years compared to earlier in your career, even though you're saving so much more?"

Brett finally capitulated. "Okay, I see your point."

Megan had a question: "This is the result under your main forecast, right? What about the alternate forecast?"

"I thought you'd never ask," said Jim as he revealed the next chart.

"This looks very similar to Figure 21 except the amounts are lower," Brett commented.

"True," said Jim, "but there is some good news. Figure 22 shows us that relatively small changes in the forecast assumptions do not lead to big changes in the overall result. That sort of stability is comforting. Planning would be very difficult if that weren't the case."

Figure 22: The future based on Jim's alternate forecast

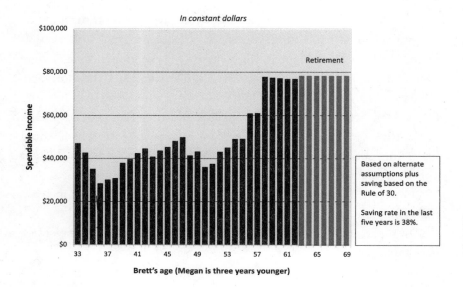

In constant dollars

Based on alternate assumptions plus saving based on the Rule of 30.

Saving rate in the last five years is 38%.

Brett's age (Megan is three years younger)

Megan kept staring at Figure 22, looking puzzled. "I don't get it, Jim. Why would the retirement income in the alternate forecast be lower than in the main forecast? After all, the real return on both stocks and bonds is higher in the alternate forecast, isn't it?"

If Jim was surprised by Megan's question, he managed not to show it. He studied the chart for a few moments as well as the spreadsheet that produced the data for the chart. The penny finally dropped, and his eyes lit up.

"Something very subtle is going on here, Megan. In the alternate forecast, the mortgage payments and work-related costs as a percentage are not dropping as quickly as in the main forecast because both wage and price inflation are lower. As a result, less money is going into the RRSP in the alternate forecast under the Rule of 30."

Megan nodded and Brett pretended he was following along.

Jim continued, "In a way, the Rule of 30 is self-correcting when it comes to inflation; can you see that? Less money is being saved when inflation is lower, but as Figure 22 shows, less saving is *needed*."

As Jim silently continued to mull over his new insight, Megan took out a folded page from her purse. It was Figure 16 from the session a month earlier. "I do have one more question," she said. "This is what you showed us back in early August. It was the projection based on what you called a 'typical' historical period, not the worst and not the best."

"You kept that?" said Jim. "Sure, I remember. It was based on the inflation rates and investment returns from 1938 to 1967."

Megan went on. "Anyway, your new forecasts look good, don't get me wrong, but they aren't anywhere nearly as good as what you called a typical past period."

Jim nodded as if to indicate he had a ready answer. "In that typical historical period, your spendable income in retirement was indeed much higher than under these new forecasts. It's partly because your real increases in pay were assumed to be higher in that prior scenario. As a result, you were creating more real wealth, which enabled you to put aside more money for retirement. In addition, the returns on both stocks and bonds were better in the period on which those numbers were based than they are in what I'm now forecasting. To put it simply, the future doesn't look as good as the past."

"That seems a shame," Megan commented. "Have you maybe been too pessimistic with your forecast assumptions?"

"It is hard to say," Jim replied. "If the future isn't as promising as the past, that's unfortunate, but the important thing is that you make the most out of it. Based on either Figure 21 or 22, that is what I think we've done."

For a few moments, no one seemed to know what else to say.

Finally, Brett spoke up. "I know you don't think your forecast is too optimistic, but is there *still* some way we could go wrong with the strategy that you've created for us?"

Jim thought about this for a moment before responding. "As I mentioned before, there could always be a black swan event, but there is no point in worrying about something like that until it happens. That aside, a few things could make the ultimate result worse than even Figure 22 suggests. First, I hate to say it, but you might divorce some day, and being single with only half as much money would make saving for retirement much more of a challenge."

At the mention of the D-word, both Brett and Megan instinctively lowered their gaze.

Megan declared, "Well, divorce is not an option; not for us."

"That's good to hear," said Jim. "But almost half of marriages do end up that way . . . even when you least expect it." He paused, looking pensive for a moment before moving on. "Second, you might find it hard to save based on the Rule of 30 because the saving percentage can vary so much from year to year due to extraordinary expenses."

Brett responded to this, "I'm the one who was initially worried about trying to save based on the Rule of 30, but I've had a chance to get used to it. I agree it should make saving easier, not harder, so it shouldn't be a problem."

"Excellent," said Jim. "Third, one or both of you could lose your job at some point close to retirement, which will make further saving a problem."

Brett again: "We spent a lot of time going through that scenario, and I thought you did a good job in convincing us we could survive it, especially if we pay off the mortgage early."

"Okay," said Jim, "And the final problem is that your children may continue to rely on hefty financial support from you, not only in your final working years but even after you retire. Stranger things have been known to happen."

Megan addressed this last issue with some firmness in her voice. "I'm going to make sure we raise our kids to be self-reliant. It'll be good for them and good for us as well."

Brett and Megan had nothing else to say. The session felt like it was coming to an end and, while the forecast wasn't as rosy as they had hoped for, they generally felt satisfied with it.

Megan said, "Well, Jim, it feels like this journey you've taken us on is coming to an end. Is it?"

"Would you be disappointed if I said yes?" Jim responded. "Actually, we are not quite done. I want to discuss some aspects of saving that could be quite important, even if you already know how much to save. After we do that, *you* can tell me if we're done!"

As Brett and Megan walked back home, Brett could tell that Megan had something on her mind.

"Poor Jim," she muttered.

"What do you mean?" asked Brett.

"That discussion about divorce seemed to have made him sad. But that's never going to happen to us, is it, Brett?"

"No chance, honey."

They walked the rest of the way home in silence, both lost in their own thoughts.

PART III

Denouement

CHAPTER 20

Rounding Out the Picture

Wednesday, September 14 and Saturday, September 17

The Wednesday night before their next session with Jim, Brett's curiosity got the better of him while he was sitting with Megan watching TV. "Hey, I thought you would have told me by now how things went when you met with Alyssa yesterday."

"Who?" Megan asked innocently.

"You know who I mean!"

"I thought you didn't want to know."

"I just don't want to get blindsided," said Brett. "So, are you going to tell me what happened?"

"Well, I posed as a customer and pretended to notice her last name for the first time as I sat down in her office. Curious coincidence, by the way, she's a redhead, like me. Anyway, I said to her, 'You know, Alyssa, it's funny but my next-door neighbour, Jim, has the same last name as you. He's an actuary.' Then she says . . ."

Brett cut her off. "Sorry, that's a little too much detail, Megan. I'm fine with the short version."

"Well, Alyssa and Jim had a falling out and she hasn't seen her dad in a few years. As time went by, it became harder to reconcile. Alyssa was afraid her dad didn't care to see her anymore, so she didn't want to make the first move. Apparently they're both stubborn."

"Go figure," said Brett.

"Anyway, I told her I was sure that her dad would love to see her. Oh, and I invited her over to dinner on Sunday night."

For the first time during the conversation, Brett looked at Megan instead of the TV screen and mused, "This ought to be interesting."

They didn't mention any of this to Jim when they saw him the next Saturday at their usual 4 p.m. time.

"Believe it or not, this is our last regular session," Jim informed them. "There will be one more short session after this, but it will be more like a graduation ceremony."

"Will we both pass?" Megan joked.

"With flying colours! Today, I want to talk about three matters that may seem like housekeeping issues, but they're actually quite important. The first one relates to choosing the appropriate retirement savings vehicle. You know how much to save, but what about *where* to save?"

"Is there really a choice?" asked Brett. "Won't all the money go into an RRSP?"

"Most of it will definitely go into an RRSP," Jim confirmed. "But remember, you can also save in a TFSA."

"A TFSA seems like a handy place to keep after-tax dollars," Brett conceded, "but I always considered it to be more like a tax-sheltered bank account. Why would we put any of our retirement savings into it if we still have tax-deductible contribution room in an RRSP?"

"There are two reasons to consider the TFSA as part of your overall retirement strategy," said Jim. "The first is that it can be a more tax-effective way to save at certain points in your career compared to an RRSP."

"How do you mean more tax-effective?" asked Brett.

"Basically, you want to maximize the value of the after-tax income you will receive in retirement from a given amount of after-tax saving. This means you want to make tax-deductible contributions to an RRSP when your marginal tax rate is high. If your marginal rate was 50 percent, for example, you get back half the money you put in as a tax refund."

"In that case, don't you always want to contribute to an RRSP instead of a TFSA?" Brett wondered. "After all, you'll always get a tax refund."

"Yes," Jim agreed, "but what if your marginal tax rate is just 25 percent when you are making your RRSP contribution and 40 percent in retirement? In that case, you'll be getting back less than you put in (ignoring, of course, the investment income that you'd earn). "Ideally, your marginal tax rate at the time you contribute to an RRSP should be higher than it will be when you start drawing an income from those savings."

"Fair enough," Brett conceded. "But is choosing between an RRSP and a TFSA important enough to make a difference to your retirement income?"

"It can be, but it's hard to show," replied Jim. "To measure the impact with precision, you would need sophisticated tax-optimization software, the type that is being developed by a firm called mygoals. If you were to use their software, it would show that you might be able to increase your after-tax dollars by maybe 10 percent by using the right vehicle at the right time. This calculation takes into account not only marginal tax rates year by year but also the impact of the OAS clawback."

"Whoa," said Megan, "how does the OAS clawback come into play?"

"Let's say you save only in RRSPs and your investments do so well that your ultimate retirement income from all sources exceeds $80,000 in today's dollars. If it does, some of your OAS pension will get clawed back. If your income is over $130,000 (once again, in today's dollars), then all of your OAS pension will get clawed back."

"Isn't it the same problem whether you save in an RRSP or a TFSA?" Brett wondered.

"Not at all," Jim replied. "Withdrawals from your TFSA are not considered income at all for tax purposes. As a result, TFSA 'income' doesn't count against you for the purposes of calculating the OAS clawback. This is one of the ways in which the TFSA can be more tax-efficient than an RRSP."

"Is there a simple way to know which vehicle we should be choosing in a given year?" asked Megan.

"In your case, you might want to do all of your saving in TFSAs in your 30s and then switch to RRSPs from age 40 and on," Jim replied. "At some point, your income might be high enough that you are maxing out on your

RRSP contributions, in which case the spillover contributions should go into a TFSA."

Then Jim suddenly had another thought. "By the way, you can use the same tax-optimization software to compare saving under the Rule of 30 to saving a flat percentage like 12 percent each year. We have already seen that the amount you accumulate on a pre-tax basis is about the same. What you really care about, though, is after-tax dollars, the money you get to keep in your pocket. On this basis, saving under the Rule of 30 wins hands down; it'll produce more after-tax income for a given amount of saving."

"Why?" Brett wondered.

"Because you end up doing most of your RRSP saving in the final third of your career, when your marginal tax rate is likely to be the highest," explained Jim.

Brett's eyes lit up. "I already liked the Rule of 30 without knowing about the tax angle, but that sounds like a nice little bonus."

Megan suddenly remembered something. "Jim, you were saying that tax efficiency was the *main* reason for splitting contributions between an RRSP and a TFSA. Is there another reason?"

"After you retire, it might be useful to have a source of income that is essentially invisible to the CRA. This idea is totally above-board, by the way, not tax evasion. As I said, withdrawals from your TFSA are not considered income at all and are therefore not taxable. As a result, TFSA dollars will go further than RRSP income, so you wouldn't have to withdraw as much to produce the same amount of spendable income as from an RRSP. Sort of like high-efficiency laundry detergent."

"And why is this tax-free income useful?"

"You never know when you may have to dig a little deeper for some emergency spending in retirement. For instance, you might want to help one of your children with the down payment on their home, or you could have a major home repair on your hands. If you withdraw a large lump sum from your RRSP, it could catapult you into a higher-income tax bracket. You can avoid that by withdrawing the necessary funds from a TFSA instead."

"Okay, good to know," Brett responded. "That's a lot to remember, but it sounds like good advice for when the time comes. Are there any other tax implications that might affect us in the short term?"

"Well, TFSA contributions do create a bit of a challenge to using the Rule of 30. When we assumed all your retirement saving went into an RRSP or a DC pension plan, I took into account the tax refund that such contributions provide. This was an integral part of the Rule of 30. If your contribution goes into a TFSA, however, there is no tax refund. If you contributed the same amount to a TFSA as you would to an RRSP, it would put you over the 30 percent threshold."

"So, what do we do?" asked Megan.

"This isn't a serious breach of the Rule of 30 because the annual TFSA contribution limit is fairly low, just $6,000 in 2021. I suggest you determine your contribution based on the Rule of 30, as usual, but then reduce that contribution by a third if the money is going into a TFSA. That approximates the tax effect."

Jim was not quite finished. "Now, you may not always have a choice between whether you save in an RRSP or a TFSA. If you participate in a workplace pension plan, the decision is made for you. Furthermore, if the workplace plan is a DC pension plan, it will typically involve a matching employer contribution. In other words, for every additional dollar that you decide to contribute, your employer makes a matching contribution on your behalf. If this situation applies to you, then you can forget everything I just said about putting money into a TFSA. You can also temporarily forget about the Rule of 30."

This had been a relatively dry session prior to this point. Indeed, Brett's attention was flagging, and even Megan looked a little more tired than usual. With Jim's last comment, however, both of them straightened up a little.

"Come again, Jim?" Brett said. "You're saying forget the Rule of 30?"

"Only in this one instance," Jim noted. "I know that neither of you participates in a workplace pension plan now, but that situation may change some day. That is why I want to talk about a special scenario.

"Let's say you're in your mid-30s with heavy daycare costs and you can barely contribute anything at all to an RRSP or a TFSA. It's for situations like this that I created the Rule of 30, in order to create a saving regime that takes into account the other expenses that are happening at various points in your life.

"Now, what if you joined a company that offered a DC pension plan? Let's say the plan *requires* employees to contribute 2 percent of pay with a matching 2 percent contributed on their behalf by the employer. Let's also assume that the plan allows employees to make optional contributions up to another 4 percent of pay, which would also be fully matched by the employer."

Brett wanted a clarification. "You're saying 4 percent of pay would go into this plan at a minimum, half of it coming from the employer. You're also saying that another 8 percent — split between me and my employer — could also go into the plan, but that it would be optional."

"That's correct," said Jim. "Maybe the mandatory 2 percent you're contributing already puts you over the Rule of 30, but since you have no choice, you don't worry about it. You do have a decision to make, about the 4 percent optional contribution, though. And remember that at this point in your lives, you are financially strapped. Do you somehow contribute that extra 4 percent of pay into this plan even though you don't know where the money is going to come from? Or do you take into account that you're already over the Rule of 30 and decide not to make any optional contribution at all, even if it means you forgo the employer matching in the process?"

Megan answered first: "Are you perhaps suggesting that we contribute the maximum, even if it takes us over 30 percent?"

"Right!"

"But why? What about the financial hardship you talked about?"

"The 'why' is easy," Jim replied. "The company is matching your contribution dollar for dollar.[1] By contributing the full 4 percent optional contribution, you are effectively getting a 4 percent raise. Better still, the company's 4 percent matching contribution isn't taxed in your hands. At least not until you retire and start drawing an income from your savings. Until then, the money grows with investment income, tax-free."

"Okay but . . ." began Megan.

Jim interrupted, "Or another way to look at it is that your 4 percent contribution earns an instant 100 percent return. In this era of near-zero interest rates, there is no way you should pass up this offer."

---

1 In some DC plans, the company match might be "only" 50 percent as much, but it would still make sense to contribute the maximum.

Megan finally got in a word. "But where will the money come from? You've already indicated we're tapped out!"

"There are two possibilities," Jim replied. "The first is to borrow the money. You can probably get a low-interest home equity loan. Normally, I wouldn't recommend borrowing in order to contribute to an RRSP or other retirement vehicle, but this is an exception.

"The other way is to reduce the amount you're paying toward your mortgage to free up some cash. This isn't always possible, but if you can somehow reduce your mortgage payments to come up with the money you need to make the optional contribution, then do so. Even if it means paying off your mortgage a little later."

Megan was frowning. "Isn't there a chance that the money we contribute to the employer's DC plan could be lost somehow? Say, if the company I work for goes under?"

"No, there's absolutely no chance of that," said Jim, "not as long as the money is invested in stocks and bonds. Just stay away from investments like GICs that are backed by second-rate financial institutions. Ironically, that type of investment can entail more risk than stocks."

It was Brett's turn now. "You're saying we do this even if it means over-saving for retirement?"

"For the foreseeable future, the answer is yes. In the long term, I'd say come back and ask me in 20 years. If you did this throughout your career, there is a chance you'd be over-saving. But the odds are that you won't stay with the employer that long; and if you do happen to be in a position in your mid-50s where you have more money than you think you'll need for retirement, then . . . ."

Brett rubbed his chin as he finished Jim's sentence. "Then it means we'll have options. We won't need to work full-time in our 60s, unless we really want to."

"Exactly. Are you both onside with this recommendation, then?" Jim asked.

Brett and Megan exchanged a glance and then looked back at Jim, nodding.

"Before we call it a day," said Jim, "I wanted to revisit a past topic, but only very briefly. Remember we looked at the question of whether it was better to rent or to buy? I regard this as more of an intellectual exercise than a practical matter, since I know you have no plans to become renters. Still, it would be interesting to see the answer based on our forecast assumptions."

Jim glanced at Megan to make sure the subject wasn't upsetting her and then continued. "You might remember Figure 14, which answered the question for past periods. It showed that from a purely financial point of view, you would have been better off renting than buying in any 30-year period that ended after 2009. Now, it's time to reveal my prediction for the next 30 years."

For some reason, Brett and Megan felt a little nervous about this.

"As you would expect, it all depends on the assumptions, but home-ownership seems to be the better bet.[2] For renting to be as good financially as owning, the returns on your portfolio would have to be at least 2 percent a year higher than what I am forecasting. Here is a list of other things that could possibly tip the decision in favour of renting:

- lower rate of appreciation on the home (versus the 1 percent annual real increase I assumed),
- higher ongoing costs for homeownership (versus the 1.25 percent of current market value that I used for insurance, property taxes and maintenance costs),
- higher mortgage interest rates (versus the 3.5 percent I've assumed after the first five years) and
- rent-to-price ratio continuing to drop (versus the 4.25 percent I assumed).

"In my mind," Jim continued, "the only thing on this list that is a real threat to homeowners is higher mortgage interest rates, and even then, the increase would have to be substantial. Bottom line, owning looks to be a little better than renting over the next 30 years. And even if it's not, owning is unlikely to be a bad decision."

Megan looked relieved. "I'm glad to hear that!"

They were all silent for a few seconds. Brett and Megan had the feeling that an important milestone had been reached.

---

2   Assumptions underlying the calculations are shown at the end of the chapter.

Finally, Jim smiled and said, "Guess what? We've reached the end of the road. How do you both feel?"

Megan spoke for both of them, "A lot better-educated and very grateful! But it's not going to end like this. We need to celebrate. Are you available for dinner tomorrow night? Say, seven o'clock?"

"Absolutely," Jim replied.

A bit more about . . .

Table 20: Assumptions used to compare renting versus buying

Mortgage interest rate (first 5 years)	2.5%
Mortgage interest rate (after 5 years)	3.5%
Purchase price of home	$450,000
Down payment	$90,000
Inflation	2.0%
Initial annual rent	$1,594
Annual increase in rent	2.0%
Real increase in home value (annual)	1.0%
Annual cost for home insurance, property taxes and maintenance (% of market value)	1.25%
Vehicle for renter's portfolio	TFSA
Investment fees on renter's portfolio	0.6%
Asset mix approach for renter's portfolio	TDF

CHAPTER 21

Graduation Day

Sunday, September 18

Fortunately, the weather was good for a barbecue the next day. Jim showed up for dinner at precisely 7 p.m. Brett and Megan had told him to come directly to the backyard, which is where he found his hosts. Brett was already heating up the barbecue while Megan was setting the table. She set it for four.

Jim didn't notice the extra place setting. He had a folder with some papers in one hand, and a bottle of champagne in the other.

"Is that what I think it is?" asked Megan.

"You mean the bubbly?" said Jim. "Well, like you said, a little celebration is in order. After tonight, our sessions are over and you can get back to your regular lives."

"But we'll still see you," Megan said, not sure if she was reassuring Jim or herself.

"I'm counting on it," Jim replied. "I don't have graduation diplomas to give you, but I did prepare this summary of the strategy that we've cobbled together over the past three months. You don't have to read it now, but I hope it'll prove useful as a reminder of how you might go about saving for retirement."

Jim gave Brett and Megan each a stapled handout entitled simply "How to save for retirement."

Megan commented, "Nice font!"

This is what was printed on the handout:

HOW TO SAVE FOR RETIREMENT

1. Save based on the "Rule of 30"

What it means: Save an amount equal to 30 percent of gross pay (combined pay in the case of a couple) less the amount you are paying toward a mortgage (or toward rent if you don't own a home) less extraordinary short-term expenses like daycare costs. If you start to save a little later in life, say after 40, you might want to increase the 30 percent a little, though the stress test shows the Rule of 30 is adequate even in this instance.

Rationale: Some people will tell you that saving for retirement is the most important thing you can do. That isn't always true, but it's still very important. This rule provides a better balance between competing priorities. It makes it simpler to decide how much to set aside each year. It is more easily doable than saving a flat percentage of pay, since there will be times in your life when saving that fixed percentage will be too onerous.

2. Follow the Rule of 30 until you're within 10 years of retirement. At that point, take stock of your retirement-readiness and adjust your saving percentage accordingly.

What it means: As you get closer to retiring, you should use a retirement calculator, such as PERC, to make final adjustments to your saving rate.

Rationale: Like any rule of thumb, the Rule of 30 is an approximation. It doesn't make sense to follow it blindly for your entire working life, since your circumstances will change over time. Your investments will do better or worse than you expected. You might lose your job or get an unexpected promotion. You might decide to push back your retirement age a few years or move it up. Using a good retirement calculator allows you to take all these circumstances, and others, into account.

3. Pay off your mortgage early.

What it means: You should always plan to pay off your mortgage by your expected retirement age at the latest. Paying it "early" means paying it off a little sooner than that; for instance, five years before you plan to retire.

Rationale: Making mortgage payments and saving for retirement are both necessary activities and, in a sense, are very similar; you're building your wealth for future use. Making mortgage payments is actually the more conservative of the two actions because the payments are made with after-tax dollars, they are not tax-deductible like the contributions to an RRSP. It makes sense to pay off the mortgage a little early because you can never tell whether your career will be curtailed. Having a paid-for house gives you one less thing to worry about.

4. Invest in stocks and bonds instead of real estate.

What it means: Buying condos or other real estate properties and renting them out has been a popular alternative to investing in stocks and bonds. As long as you have contribution room in an RRSP or TFSA, the use of tax-assisted investment vehicles is a better bet.

Rationale: My analysis shows that one is highly unlikely to do better going the real estate route.

5. Use a target-date-fund (TDF) approach to set your asset mix.

What it means: Whether you use target date funds or keep adjusting your asset mix manually, start with a high equity weighting (up to 100 percent) in your portfolio when you are young and gradually increase the bond weighting to an ultimate mix of 50-50 just before retirement. If you are comfortable with buying and selling ETFs, you might want to do it manually, since the investment management fees are likely to be lower.

Rationale: The TDF approach has been more effective than a 60-40 asset mix over 30-year periods. Based on the forecasted returns for stocks and bonds, it is expected to remain more effective in the future. The slow increase in the bond weighting guards against a large loss just before retirement in case there is a sudden, severe drop in stock prices.

6. Pick the right retirement saving vehicle.

What it means: Unless you are lucky enough to participate in a workplace pension plan, you will be saving primarily through RRSPs and TFSAs. When your marginal tax rate is lower, you should make maximum use of TFSAs, to the extent you have contribution room; and when it is higher, you should use RRSPs.

Rationale: Because of their different tax characteristics, there is a place for both RRSPs and TFSAs. Having money in both might also confer some advantages during the decumulation period, depending on your tax situation.

7. Don't borrow money to save for retirement *unless* you participate in a workplace pension plan and your contributions attract employer matched contributions.

What it means: Borrowing to save is one way to mitigate the pain of saving during lean years, but it's not generally recommended. The exception is when you can make optional contributions to a workplace DC pension plan and those optional contributions are matched by employer contributions.

Rationale: A matching employer contribution is like getting an instant 100 percent return on your money. This is always valuable but especially in a low-interest era.

Megan held it out admiringly and offered, "Nice summary, Jim. If you had to boil it down to one basic thought for us to remember, what would that be?"

Jim thought about it before answering, "It's important to save for retirement, but there is much more to life than retirement. You should be able to enjoy every phase, and that should be easier to do if you save in a way that spreads out the pain over the entire accumulation period."

Brett and Megan nodded appreciatively.

There was a lull in the conversation, which prompted Jim to ask, "Any final questions?"

Brett responded for them, "No, that pretty much covers it. We don't know how to thank you, Jim."

"Don't mention it," Jim replied. "I'm glad if you found this exercise useful. It was for me, too, since it clarified my thinking on a number of fronts. Even actuaries don't know all this stuff off the top of their heads!"

Jim then popped the cork off the champagne. As he started to fill the glasses, Megan said, "Sorry, Jim, but I think I'll stick with ginger ale."

Jim raised his eyebrows. "Are you saying what I think you're saying?"

"Yes, we found out a few weeks ago. I had an ultrasound the other day and they told us things are going well. It's a boy!" she exclaimed, her face beaming.

"Congratulations! When is the baby due?"

"Late March," Megan answered. "I believe that's a couple of months ahead of the actuarial projection you made for us?"

"Yes, I guess it is. I'm so pleased for both of you. Have you picked a name?"

Megan looked at Brett and then back at Jim. "We're thinking of calling him James."

For once in his life, Jim was at a loss for words.

After clearing his throat, he finally said, "Aren't you full of surprises!"

Megan casually responded, "You think? Oh, by the way. I hope you don't mind, but I invited someone else to join us tonight for dinner."

"Anyone I know?"

"I think so."

At that moment, a red-headed young lady could be spotted coming around the corner.

CHAPTER 22

The Big Picture

The primary goal of saving for retirement is to have enough to "retire comfortably," however you might define that state of being. But if that is all you seek to do, you are setting the bar too low. How you save is nearly as important as how much you save.

Consider Figure 23, for instance. It shows what would have happened had a couple started to save in 1990 when they were in their early 30s, saved 10 percent a year and retired at the start of 2020 when the older spouse was 63. We will call this the 10-percent scenario.[1] (Note that this chart is expressed in constant 2020 dollars.)

There is nothing wrong with the ultimate result under this 10-percent scenario. Spendable income in the couple's retirement compares quite favourably to spendable income in their final working years. But notice that spendable income dips below $25,000 in two of the early working years, compared to nearly $120,000 (in real terms) after retirement. It would have been much better if the couple had managed to reach the same goal without so much sacrifice.

---

1   Details on this projection are given at the end of the chapter.

Figure 23: Saving 10 percent since 1990 and retiring in 2019

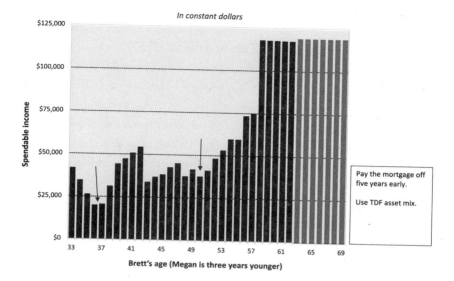

In constant dollars

Spendable income

Brett's age (Megan is three years younger)

Pay the mortgage off five years early.

Use TDF asset mix.

If they had saved using the Rule of 30, they would have achieved the result shown in Figure 24. While spendable income in retirement is virtually the same as under the 10-percent scenario, the Rule of 30 requires much less

Figure 24: Saving from 1990–2019 with the Rule of 30

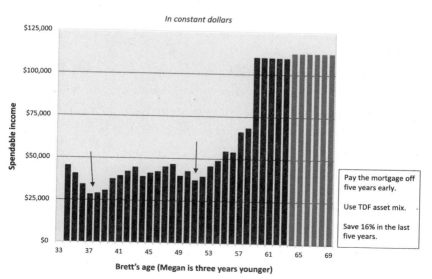

In constant dollars

Spendable income

Brett's age (Megan is three years younger)

Pay the mortgage off five years early.

Use TDF asset mix.

Save 16% in the last five years.

sacrifice during the early years. In the worst years — ages 36 and 37 — spendable income under the Rule of 30 scenario is at least 40 percent greater.

Therefore, the secondary goal in saving for retirement is maintaining a comfortable level of spendable income throughout your working years. Ideally, spendable income should be steadily rising in real terms as pre-tax income rises. It should reach its highest level just before retirement and then remain at (or very near) that high level in all subsequent years. This result is difficult to achieve because life's major events intervene, such as having children and buying homes. Nevertheless, the Rule of 30 enables savers to come closer to achieving this pattern than by saving a flat percentage of pay.

This brings us to the last chart in this book. Figure 25, which breaks down all spending into just four major categories, serves to clarify the importance of the Rule of 30. One of those four categories is fixed costs, meaning the sum of (a) what we spend to raise our children, (b) work-related expenses and (c) income tax. Strictly speaking, these costs are not totally fixed, since we can decide whether and when to have children, how much we will spend on them and how we will commute to work, but it helps to think of these costs as a fixed number.

By contrast, the amount we pay for our home can be quite variable. We can choose how much house we buy, how quickly we want to pay off the mortgage and even whether to rent instead.

The other two categories shown in the chart are retirement saving and what I call "spendable income," which is a catch-all for everything else we spend money on in our lives.

As Figure 25 shows, all spending and saving is interrelated. If you buy more house, it will crowd out either your spendable income or your retirement saving or both. The same goes with retirement saving. If you make that another fixed cost, say, by saving a constant 10 or 12 percent a year, you must then cut spending elsewhere.

Sometimes you get lucky. For instance, if investment returns are especially good (which was the case from 1990 to 2019), you can reduce your saving rate and therefore increase your spendable income. More likely, spendable income has to be squeezed to make room to save enough. Making sacrifices and cutting corners is always doable, especially when you're younger, but there are limits to what one should tolerate. The Rule

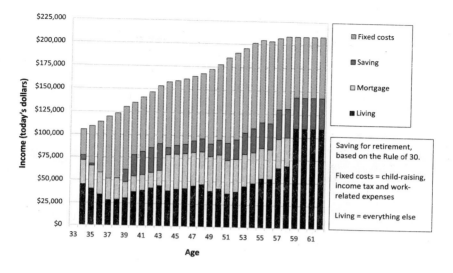

Figure 25: A spending breakdown under the Rule of 30

Legend:
- Fixed costs
- Saving
- Mortgage
- Living

Saving for retirement, based on the Rule of 30.

Fixed costs = child-raising, income tax and work-related expenses

Living = everything else

Y-axis: Income (today's dollars)
X-axis: Age

of 30 attempts to reduce the amount of sacrifice that is needed. It aims to make this balancing act more manageable by allowing three of the four categories — mortgage payments, spendable income and retirement savings — to vary year by year as circumstances dictate.

The strategy that is best for you may ultimately come down to a question of personality. If you are very conservative, you might still want to save 10 or 12 percent of pay every year, come hell or high water, because you find the thought of under-saving to be unbearable. If you are both disciplined and rational, you might prefer the Rule of 30 for all the reasons given above. To paraphrase Jim, if the Rule of 30 allows you to achieve your primary saving goal with less pain, why would you do anything else?

In closing, the astute reader will notice that we didn't answer the question that was posed in Chapter 1 — how much to save for retirement? If I absolutely had to provide a one-size-fits-all flat percentage of pay, I would make it 12 percent with the caveat that you might have to change that percentage as you get closer to retirement. If I could express it differently, I would suggest saving 5 percent of pay in your thirties, 15 percent in your 40s and 25 percent in your 50s. This alternative represents a rough approximation of the Rule of 30.

In reality, no one percentage or set of percentages can be certain to carry most savers across the finish line safely without causing undue hardship along the way. In this case, the old cliché is true: The journey is indeed as important as the destination.

A bit more about . . .

Table 21: Details underlying Figures 23 and 24

	Saving 10%/year	Saving based on the Rule of 30
Age of the couple in 1990	33 and 30	Same
Combined pay in 1990	$60,000	Same
When homes were bought	Start of year 1 and year 11	Same
When mortgage is paid off	Five years before retirement	Same
Asset mix during accumulation	Target-date-fund approach	Same
Savings rate in last five years	10%	15%
How retirement income is optimized	Using PERC	Using PERC

APPENDIX

Pensions from Government Sources

Canadians with employment earnings can expect to receive a pension from the Canada or Quebec Pension Plan (CPP or QPP). Every Canadian with at least 10 years of residency after age 18 is also entitled to an Old Age Security (OAS) pension.

As Jim showed in Figure 2 (Chapter 3), government pensions are an important source of retirement income for middle-income Canadians. Because of the recent expansion of the Canada Pension Plan, it will become even more important in the years to come. When estimating your saving rate and projected retirement income, it is highly recommended that these pensions be included.

CPP or QPP?

Quebec workers contribute to the Quebec Pension Plan (QPP). People employed in the rest of Canada contribute to the Canada Pension Plan (CPP). The CPP and QPP provide essentially the same pension benefits. They also used to require the same level of contributions but, due to poorer demographic and investment experience in Quebec, the QPP has required higher contributions for the past few years and will continue to do so.[1] This appendix will focus specifically on the CPP but with the understanding that the same information (apart from contributions) applies broadly to the QPP as well.

CPP Expansion

On June 20, 2016, then Finance Minister Bill Morneau announced the biggest change to the CPP in half a century. The program was expanded to provide significantly greater pensions . . . eventually. The change was made official on March 3, 2017, with the first increase in contribution rates occurring in 2019.

The expansion of CPP affects only contributions made, and pension benefits earned, from 2019 and on. Indeed, the higher CPP benefits due to expansion will not be fully phased in until about 2070. The expansion, therefore, has little or no impact on current retirees or on those retiring in the next few years. It is a different story for Brett and Megan. The impact of the expansion was factored into the pension projections that Jim performed for Brett and Megan, as their retirement horizon is 30 years out, when the expansion will be well under way. Details are given below.

A Bird's-Eye View of the Impact

Before 2019, the CPP provided a maximum pension equal to 25 percent of earnings up to a ceiling that approximates the national average wage. This is the pre-expansion benefit and assumes the worker contributed the maximum amount to the CPP for most of his career and started CPP at 65. The maximum pension payable in 2019 to someone who turned 65 that year was $1,154.58 a month.

---

[1]   The maximum employee contribution in 2020 was $2,898 to the CPP and $3,146.40 to the QPP.

Once the CPP expansion is fully phased in, the CPP will provide a maximum pension equal to 33.33 percent of pensionable earnings versus the previous 25 percent, once again assuming commencement at age 65; it will be more or less than that if the pension starts later or earlier.

This higher benefit rate will apply on earnings up to a ceiling that will be 14 percent higher than the old ceiling. As a result, the revised maximum pension will be about 52 percent bigger[2] than if the rules had not been changed. A worker will still have had to contribute at the maximum level for most of her career to earn the maximum. But now, because of the higher ceiling, it will be more difficult to do.

To fund the higher pension, workers and employers must both contribute more. The higher contributions are being phased in starting in 2019 with the phase-in completed by 2025. The extra cost is split 50-50 between employees and employers.

Details on Contributions

CPP participants are required to contribute based on their employment earnings between ages 18 and 65. If they have earnings between ages 65 and 70 and they choose to defer the start of their CPP pensions, they must continue to contribute after age 65. Participants who have started their CPP pensions by age 65 do not have to contribute after age 65, even if they still have pensionable earnings, but they may choose to do so and earn additional pension credits.

The contribution rules below apply to employees, with employers making a matching contribution. In the case of self-employed persons, the contribution rate is double that shown.

Before the expansion, workers contributed 4.95 percent of their employment earnings between the Year's Basic Exemption (YBE) and the Year's Maximum Pensionable Earnings (YMPE). The YBE is a constant $3,500 of earnings and is not expected to change. The YMPE in 2018 — the year before the phase-in of the expanded pension began — was $55,900. Hence, the maximum employee contribution that year was $2,593.80.

---

2    $33.33 / 25 \times 1.14 = 1.52$

In 2019, the contribution rate was increased to 5.10 percent. The YMPE in 2019 was $57,400 and was unaffected by the CPP expansion. As before, the YMPE continues to rise annually by the percentage change in the national average wage, rounded down to the nearest $100. The table below shows both the actual and expected contribution rates as a result of the expansion of the CPP. (*Amounts in italics are estimates.*)

Year	Contribution rate[3]	Earnings ceiling (YMPE)[4]	Maximum contribution*
2019	5.10%	$57,400	$2,774.40
2020	5.25%	$58,700	$2,898.00
2021	5.45%	$61,600	$3,166.45
2022	5.70%	*$63,400*	*$3,414.30*
2023	5.95%	*$65,300*	*$3,677.10*

*Double for self-employed persons

After 2023, the contribution rate up to the YMPE remains at 5.95 percent for both employees and employers. The YBE will remain at $3,500 and the YMPE will continue to rise in line with increases in the national average wage.

A second phase of the CPP expansion commences in 2024, with the addition of a new contribution limit, known as the Year's Additional Maximum Pensionable Earnings, or YAMPE for short. Employees and employers will each be required to contribute 4 percent of earnings between the YMPE and the YAMPE.

In 2024, the YAMPE will be 107 percent of the YMPE. Since the YMPE is estimated to be $67,200 in 2024, the YAMPE is estimated to be $71,900. In 2025, the YAMPE will be approximately $78,900, which represents 114 percent of the YMPE. After 2025, the YAMPE will continue to increase in line with the national average wage, the same as the YMPE.[5]

---

3   On employment earnings in excess of the YBE.

4   The ceiling for years beyond 2021 is an estimate only.

5   More specifically, by the increase in the 12-month average of the weekly earnings of the industrial aggregate since June 30 of the previous year, rounded down to the next lower multiple of $100.

The amount equal to 4.95 percent of pensionable earnings up to the YMPE is known as the **Base Contribution**. The extra amount (due to both the higher percentage contributed and the higher contribution ceiling as described above) is known as the **Additional Contribution**. It should be noted that contributing employees receive a tax credit rather than a tax deduction for their Base Contribution. By contrast, the Additional Contribution is fully tax-deductible, which is a much more favourable tax treatment for higher-income earners.

Note that the employee contribution rate on earnings up to the YMPE is 5.95 percent versus 4 percent between the YMPE and YAMPE even though the benefit accrual rate is the same (33.33 percent of earnings). If participants were paying a fair price for their CPP pension, the contribution rate should be the same on both tranches of earnings. The nearly 1.95 percent difference in contribution rate between the two tranches reflects a legacy cost.

In the early days of the CPP, the first retirees were granted a full CPP benefit after as few as 10 years of contributions. Moreover, they were contributing just 1.8 percent of earnings up to a very low ceiling, lower even than the average wage of the day. In other words, the benefit they received was much greater than what they paid into the program.

That "gift" to the CPP's early participants came at a price for everyone else contributing to the plan. It is the reason why employees and employers will each have to contribute an extra 1.95 percent of pay (on contributions up to the YMPE) into perpetuity. It is not clear why the decision to grant this gift should have been left in the hands of politicians when it is the workers and their employers who bear the entire cost of the plan. When it comes to matters of intergenerational equity, no one is on hand to speak for future generations!

Pension Benefits

The portion of the CPP pension based on the rules in effect before 2019 is known as the **Base CPP**. The maximum Base CPP (assuming retirement at age 65) is essentially 25 percent of the average YMPE in the year of pension commencement and the four preceding years; but to achieve the full

25 percent, one has to contribute the maximum amount to the plan for 40 years. (The reason why one isn't required to contribute the maximum amount for the full 47 years between ages 18 and age 65 is given below under "Dropout Rules.")

The portion of the CPP pension due to the expansion is known as the **Additional CPP**. The total maximum CPP pension at age 65 for a contributor is 33.33 percent of the average YAMPE in the year of pension commencement and the previous four years. The Additional CPP therefore consists of the additional pension due to the higher benefit accrual rate (33.33 percent versus 25 percent) and also the higher pensionable earnings ceiling (up to the YAMPE versus the YMPE). Put another way, the Additional CPP is the difference between the total CPP pension (post-enhancement) and the Base CPP. For contributors who retire between now and 2070, their CPP pension will be a blend of the old rules and the new rules. Retirees in the next few years are barely affected by the expansion.

The formula for calculating Additional CPP pension benefits can be broken down into two parts. The first part is 8.33 percent of additional monthly pensionable earnings up to the adjusted YMPE. During the phase-in years of 2019 to 2022, however, it will be a lower percentage because the contribution rate is less than 5.95 percent in those years. Specifically, the additional accrual rate (rounded) will be as follows in those years:

2019	1.25%
2020	2.5%
2021	4.17%
2022	6.25%

The second part of the additional pension is 33.33 percent of additional monthly pensionable earnings between the YMPE and the YAMPE.

Ultimate Impact of the Expansion

When the new CPP rules are fully phased in, the impact of the expansion could be very significant. For example, assume that the national average wage rises by 3 percent a year until 2065. In that case, the maximum CPP pension, payable from age 65, will be $80,100 under the new rules versus $52,700 if the CPP had not been enhanced.[6] These figures are expressed in estimated 2065 dollars.

As already noted, not many Canadians will earn the maximum CPP pension because it would require earnings that are 14 percent higher than the national average wage from one's mid-20s until age 65. To earn the maximum CPP pension under the new rules, a participant who turns 25 in 2025, the first year of full contributions, would have to earn at least $78,900 that year plus ever-higher amounts (to reflect wage inflation) in every subsequent year until age 65.

Early Commencement

A contributor can choose to start his CPP pension as early as age 60. If he continues to have pensionable earnings after early commencement of CPP, he will be required to continue contributing and could earn additional retirement benefits. There is, however, a penalty for early commencement of CPP pension: 0.6 percent for each month that commencement precedes age 65 (7.2 percent a year or 36 percent if CPP pension commences at age 60). Also, the CPP pension on early retirement would be based on the YMPE and YAMPE levels at the time of retirement (and the four preceding years), not the levels at age 65.

Postponed Commencement

Participants can elect to defer their CPP pension until age 70. If they defer commencement beyond age 65, the starting pension is increased by 0.7 percent for each month (8.4 percent for each year) that commencement is deferred. In addition, the CPP pension will be based on the YMPE and

---

6   We'll ignore the fact that the YMPE and YAMPE are both rounded down to the nearest $100 each year.

YAMPE levels in the year of commencement and four preceding years, not when the participant turned 65.

As a result, the maximum CPP payable to someone who defers commencement to age 70 can be more than 42 percent greater than at 65. If wage inflation exceeds price inflation by 1 percent a year, for example, the pension at 70 will be 49.2 percent higher than at 65, plus the effect of inflation in the intervening period. Very few CPP contributors take advantage of these postponed commencement rules, but it is generally in the best interests of participants to defer their CPP to age 70.[7]

If a participant defers CPP to 70 and has no earnings between 65 and 70, those five years of no earnings do not count against her in determining the amount of pension payable.

Dropout Rules

Someone starting their CPP pension at age 65 would be required to contribute between ages 18 and 65, or 47 years in total. However, for purposes of calculating the amount of CPP pension payable at age 65, only the best 40 years would count, as one could "drop out" the seven years[8] with the lowest earnings relative to the YMPE and YAMPE. Anyone with an eligible disability or with time off from work due to rearing children under the age of seven could have additional years included in the dropout period.

To be clear, one cannot receive more than the maximum CPP pension even if they have contributed for more than the required 40 years or if they are entitled to a surviving spouse pension in addition to their own pension. (As an aside, this cap is akin to the limit on the speed of light; you simply cannot exceed it even when you think you should.) Moreover, one is required to contribute up until age 65 even if one has already contributed enough to receive the maximum pension.

---

7   There are exceptions. This subject is covered at length in the book *Retirement Income for Life*.

8   Actually, it is based on 18 percent of the contributory period, which is 7.99 years at age 65 and 7.56 years at age 60.

Impact for Brett and Megan

We will assume that Brett is 33 and Megan is 30 as of December 15, 2021. We will also assume that their best 40 years of earnings for CPP pension purposes are their last 40 up until retirement.

Because they are expected to retire in 30 years, their CPP pensions could start in January 2052, when Brett is 63 and Megan is 60. Since Brett always had earnings above both the YMPE and in future above the YAMPE, he will earn the maximum pension but only to the extent that the CPP expansion has been phased in by 2052. In other words, he earned the maximum under the old rules for the years before 2019 plus the maximum under the expansion rules from 2019 and on, so his ultimate pension is a blend of the old and new rules.

His Base CPP pension as of 2052 would be the maximum at that time, which is estimated to be $35,230 per annum if he were age 65 then (he's actually 63). This figure would then be reduced by 0.6 percent monthly if he takes early CPP pension, or be increased by 0.7 percent for each month he defers commencement beyond 65.

His Additional CPP pension, again payable if he were 65, would be $13,551. This represents an increase over the Base CPP of 38.5 percent. Since the maximum increase in CPP is 52 percent once the expansion is fully phased in, Brett will be entitled to about 75 percent of the expanded benefits.

In Megan's case, the increase would be smaller, since her earnings in the earlier years were less than either the YMPE or the YAMPE. If her earnings at age 30 were $44,000, her estimated Base CPP pension in 2052 would be $32,274. Her estimated Additional CPP pension would be $11,615, which represents an increase of 36 percent versus no expansion. As with Brett, these amounts would be adjusted up or down depending on whether she starts her CPP later or earlier than age 65.

Old Age Security Pension

As of January 1, 2021, the maximum OAS pension for an individual who started payments at age 65 is $615.37 a month. One needs to have been resident in Canada for 40 years after age 18 to receive the maximum, otherwise the pension is pro-rated. OAS pension rises quarterly in step with increases in the Consumer Price Index. Since wages tend to rise faster than general prices, this means that OAS pensions are slowly shrinking in importance for the average Canadian. For example, the current OAS pension is about 12 percent of the current average wage. In 30 years' time, it will be less than 9 percent of the average wage; another reason why the CPP expansion was needed.

The only significant change to OAS pensions since the early 1970s was the introduction of the clawback in the 1980s. If you were 65 in 2021 and had income over $79,845 in that year, you would have to pay back some of the OAS pension you were receiving. OAS income is essentially "clawed back" at the rate of 15 percent of your income that is in excess of $79,845. You would receive no benefit at all from OAS pensions if your earnings were over $129,000 in 2021.

There are some ways to mitigate the clawback. If your income is going to be high only for a few years after 65, you might be better off to defer the start date of your OAS pension until age 70. While it means you'll wait five years longer to receive OAS, that won't matter if the full amount of OAS pension would have been clawed back in those first five years of retirement anyway. As a bonus, the starting amount if you start OAS at 70 would be 36 percent higher than taking it at 65, and maybe by then the extra income that was causing OAS to be clawed back would no longer be a factor.

Another strategy involves drawing more of your retirement income from your TFSA or non-registered savings that you may have and drawing less from taxable sources. TFSA withdrawals are not deemed to be "income" for tax purposes and don't count for clawback purposes. Similarly, if you are drawing down the capital from non-registered savings, the amounts received are not deemed to be income, assuming tax has already been paid on any capital gains that those savings had earned over the years.

ACKNOWLEDGEMENTS

My heartfelt thanks to:

Market research consultant and wife Michelle Massie for providing moral, intellectual and nutritional support as I wrote the book.

Retired actuary and pension guru Malcolm Hamilton for his help with the economic forecast and other key aspects of the book.

RBC investment advisor Franco Barbiero for extending his research resources as needed.

Nephew and future tech billionaire Christopher Vettese for fixing my computer when I really needed it.

Mad Men advertising executive Ed Caffyn for his insights into what it's like to be a landlord.

My ever-supportive friends at LifeWorks (formerly Morneau Shepell), under the leadership of Stephen Liptrap, and my new friends at Purpose Investments, under the leadership of Som Seif.

ECW Press executive Jennifer Smith for being a super-supportive publisher; and the extensive and capable team that surrounds her, including Karen Milner, Samantha Chin and Susannah Ames.

INDEX

Figures and tables indicated by page numbers in italics

stock market
  being fully invested vs. market
    timing, 89–92, *91*
  demographics and, 150–51
  equity risk premiums (ERPs) and,
    154
  exchange-traded funds (ETFs),
    88–89, 138, 183
  forecasting, 149–55, *155*
  historical performance, 10–13, *13*,
    77–79, 150
  inside information, 88
  management fees, 56, 183
  mutual funds, 88, 138
  price-to-earnings ratios (P/E
    ratios), 151–54, *152*
  real returns, 77–79, 150–51
  stock picking, 88
  See also bonds; investing

target date funds (TDFs) approach,
  82–85, *83*, 87, 89, 155, 183
tax, income, 30, *30*, 31–32, 42, 110, 172–74
Tax-Free Savings Account (TFSA),
  172–75, 183–84
T. Rowe Price, 6

undue weight vs. reversion to the
  mean, 127–28
United Kingdom, 79
United States of America, 6, 78–79, 142,
  146

Vettese, Frederick
  Retirement Income for Life, 19, 56

wages. *See* salaries and wages
Walker, Michael, 146
work-related expenses, 30, *30*

FREDERICK VETTESE is Canada's most visible actuary. His entire career has been focused on working within Canada's retirement income system. For 27 years, he was chief actuary of Morneau Shepell, a Canadian HR services firm with 6,000 employees and 24,000 clients. Vettese now spends most of his professional time speaking and writing about retirement issues. He has written over 100 articles and op-eds for the *Globe and Mail* and the *National Post* alone. He is the author of the #1 bestseller *Retirement Income for Life*, published by ECW Press. He lives in Toronto, Ontario.